everyone
is a
customer

everyone
is a
customer

A PROVEN METHOD FOR
MEASURING THE VALUE OF
EVERY RELATIONSHIP
IN THE ERA OF
COLLABORATIVE BUSINESS

Jeffrey Shuman and Janice Twombly
with David Rottenberg
THE RHYTHM OF BUSINESS, INC.

A **Kaplan Professional** Company

Vice President and Publisher: Cynthia A. Zigmund
Editorial Director: Donald J. Hull
Senior Acquisitions Editor: Jean Iversen
Senior Managing Editor: Jack Kiburz
Interior Design: Lucy Jenkins
Cover Design: Jody Billert, Billert Communications
Typesetting: the dotted i

The Purposeful Collaboration Process is patent pending by The Rhythm of Business, Inc. The Rhythm of Business is a registered trademark of The Rhythm of Business, Inc.

© 2002 by The Rhythm of Business, Inc.

Published by Dearborn Trade Publishing, a Kaplan Professional Company

Printed in the United States of America

02 03 04   10 9 8 7 6 5 4 3 2 1

Library of Congress Cataloging-in-Publication Data

Shuman, Jeffrey C., 1945–
    Everyone is a customer : a proven method for measuring the value of every relationship in the era of collaborative business / Jeffrey Shuman and Janice Twombly, with David Rottenberg.
        p.   cm.
    Includes bibliographical references and index.
    ISBN 0-7931-5412-X
    1. Customer relations.   I. Twombly, Janice.   II. Rottenberg, David, 1946– III. Title.
    HF5414.5 S554   2002
    658.8'12—dc21   2002002864

OTHER BOOKS BY THE AUTHORS

Collaborative Communities: Partnering for Profit in the Networked Economy, Dearborn Trade, 2001

The Rhythm of Business: The Key to Building and Running Successful Companies, Butterworth-Heinemann, 1998

Venture Feasibility Planning Guide (with Robert Ronstadt), Lord Publishing, Inc., 1988

DEDICATION

In memory of our fathers, Max Shuman, David Twombly, and
Myer Rottenberg, for showing us the importance of relationships

■ **You increasingly have** to think through what relationships make the most sense—the customer is the most important relationship.

Peter Drucker
Keynote Speech Collaborative Commerce Summit
June 2001

CONTENTS

Part Three   Choreographing Your Success

ACKNOWLEDGMENTS

We could never have written this book without the support and collaboration we received from a number of very special relationships.

Clearly, this book would not have been possible without the thoughtful contributions of David Rottenberg, our editor at The Rhythm of Business, Inc., and valued collaborator in all our writing.

We are sure this book would still be incomplete and poorer in content without the professional guidance of our friend and colleague David Blakelock. Not only did he help us think through the methodology we've written about in this book, but he tirelessly nurtured the creation of RelationsWeb, the first and only software that allows you to measure and manage the value of relationship currencies.

Heartfelt thanks to Gordie Earle of Arrayworks for helping us understand the requirements of the information infrastructure that support collaborative relationships.

A special thanks to Sonja Ali, who assists us in getting the words out by managing our marketing communications and our speaking and training engagements. And to Ana Hicks for her considerable skills in helping us build our community.

Stephanie Pierce-Conway's design talent allowed us to see and illustrate our process for valuing relationships.

A special thanks to Frank Bernhard, Lisa Dennis, Irwin Heller, Andrew Merken, R. David Newton, Richard Slifka, and Fred Tuffile, whose partnerships have helped us understand what it takes to build collaborative relationships.

We offer our gratitude to our customers, friends, and supporters, who in many cases have allowed us to share their stories: Doug Adams, Jon Aram, Christina Bauer, John Bastow, Stephen Berman, Eric Bobby, Dale Boch, Buddy Carp, Warren Cohen, Fred Dearman, Tim DeMello, John Dewitt, Sherri Dorfman, Ann Fazio, David Fialkow, Jay Fialkow, Ellen Fanning, Darcy Fowkes, Lisa Guyon, Kari Johnson, Larry Kaye, John Kenney, John Tae Kim, Julia King, Tom Koulopoulos, Janet Kraus, John Ladge, Miroslav Maramica, Kevin McCall, Nathaniel Palmer, Chris Pisapia, Jeff Reichenthal, Carol Rozwell, Bob Russell, Carol Russell, Jerry Socol, Laurence Stybel, Teddy Tijan, Greg Walsh, Travis White, Jason Wong, and Joe Zarrett.

Our special relationship with Bentley College is enriched by the unstinting support of Tony Buono, Pat Flynn, Charles Hadlock, Vicki LaFarge, Janet Mendelsohn, Joe Morone, Aaron Nurick, Lee Schlorff, John Seeger, and Hans Thamhain. In addition, hundreds of Bentley Entrepreneurship students continue to sharpen our thinking with their questions and their answers!

The enthusiastic support of our agent, Doris Michaels, and her staff helped our manuscript find a truly innovative publisher.

Jean Iversen, Dearborn Trade's senior acquisitions editor, and the rest of the team at Dearborn Trade made indispensable contributions to the finished book.

And none of this would have been possible without the love and support of Jeff's family—Penny, Rachel, and Alison Shuman.

PREFACE

e began both of our previous books with a quote from Peter Drucker—considered by many to be *the* foremost management thinker of the 20th century. So naturally we were thrilled to have the great privilege of meeting Peter Drucker and speaking on the same stage during the Delphi Group's Collaborative Commerce Summit in June 2001.

What has always separated Professor Drucker from the rest of the business thinkers is his ability to present complex ideas in simple, easy-to-understand terms. He just makes sense.

Our first book, *The Rhythm of Business: The Key to Building and Running Successful Companies*, quotes from Professor Drucker's landmark book *Innovation and Entrepreneurship* (Harper and Row, 1985) to emphasize a basic truth of entrepreneurship:

> When a new venture does succeed, more often than not it is in a market other than the one it was originally intended to serve, with products or services not quite those with which it had set out, bought in large part by

customers it did not even think of when started, and used for a host of purposes besides the ones for which the products were first designed.

Clearly, Professor Drucker is making a very profound and very important point. Most businesspeople do not succeed by bringing into reality the idea with which they began. Why? Because every business goes through a natural development process that we call "the rhythm of business." And our book *The Rhythm of Business* focuses on identifying and describing this iterative development process and on explaining how all natural-born entrepreneurs intuitively use this process to build and run successful companies.

At the start of the 21st century, when we wrote our second book, we knew we were living at a time when a major technological development was sweeping the globe—the shift to the networked economy, where anyone could be instantaneously connected to anyone else. It was obvious that this major event necessitated a change in business patterns. Communication and information technologies were producing more powerful consumers who wanted their needs satisfied more personally. And simultaneously the same communication and information technologies were providing businesses with the means to satisfy those personal needs. But how? What new business patterns and structures were emerging?

Our second book, *Collaborative Communities: Partnering for Profit in the Networked Economy*, attempts to answer these questions. And once again Peter Drucker's astute observations stated in an interview with James Daly in the August 2000 issue of *Business 2.0* echo our views: "The corporation as we know it, which is now 120 years old, is unlikely to survive the next 25 years. Legally and financially yes, but not structurally and economically."

Collaborative Communities explains in detail how to build a new business structure that allows companies to satisfy the personal needs and wants of their customers by establishing a network of business partners. In the book we challenge the most deeply held 20th-century assumptions about achieving success in business and demonstrate in a step-by-step fashion how to organize a 21st-century business around customers in collaboration with business partners. Regardless of how long you've been in business and no matter how many customers you have or what your company's revenues and profits are, it is our belief that you must embrace the Collaborative Community as *the* business pattern for achieving success in today's networked economy.

PEARLS BY PETER

When we met Professor Drucker at the Collaborative Commerce Summit, we were elated. And as you might expect, even at age 92, Peter still delivers "pearls of wisdom." Quite honestly, we came away from his 90-minute presentation impressed with his grasp of what it takes for success in the 21st century.

Included among his dozen or so pearls is one in particular that addresses exactly the focus of our current research: *"You increasingly have to think through what relationships make the most sense—the customer is the most important relationship."*

Thus, when we started writing *Everyone Is a Customer*, we again realized we could use Peter's eloquently stated ideas to reinforce our views.

The notion that "you increasingly have to think through what relationships make the most sense" is the focus of this book. In it, we describe a methodology whereby you allocate resources to those relationships that provide you with the greatest value.

However, given our very changed business environment and its resulting impact on the conduct of business, we see this book's challenge in a more general sense as trying to answer a simple but fundamental question: How do you do business in the era of collaborative business?

As you read, we believe the answer will become clear.

Enjoy the dance!

Jeffrey Shuman and Janice Twombly
Newton, Massachusetts
February 2002

INTRODUCTION

Collaboration may be the most important concept in business today. A recent search for the term on the Internet turned up thousands and thousands of business-related references. Yet in March 2000, while researching our last book, *Collaborative Communities: Partnering for Profit in the Networked Economy*, a similar online search came up with just a few references, and they mainly related to cooperative housing and academic or intellectual collaboration.

So why the sudden attention to collaboration? The answer is simple.

Collaboration is important because we live our lives and conduct our business in an increasingly connected and interdependent world. Collaboration is how work gets done when we can't get it done alone. In our personal lives as consumers, whenever we have the financial wherewithal, we rely on an increasing number of specialists to help us with our needs. In war, we form alliances for very specific advantages. In business, more and more companies understand that to truly succeed in our global and networked economy, growth and profits come through true partnerships with all our varied constituencies.

Indeed, many businesspeople are realizing that significant financial benefits accrue through collaborative relationships with other businesses. And increasingly companies are finding that the best strategy is to collaborate with their customers in the design, development, and delivery of their market basket of goods and services.

So not surprisingly, many businesses have essentially made collaboration their new corporate mandate. It's as if all you need to do is implement software that allows you to conduct "collaborative commerce" and you're on the road to success. However, it is our view that to be effective, collaboration requires both a mindset nurtured and developed by an entrepreneurial focus on the customer and the support of technology that provides real-time information and measurements. Collaboration must have a clearly defined purpose. Collaboration driven just by the ability of tools or by the management concept du jour results only in costly failures. Unfortunately, based on what we see and hear, in too many instances it is the superficial approach that is being taken.

Since writing *Collaborative Communities*, we have worked with dozens of companies to develop collaborative business models, all the while building our own Collaborative Community. And whether using the entrepreneurial clean sheet of paper to start a new business or iterating an existing business model, we have observed and experienced firsthand the myriad challenges to building a collaborative business.

Lately, we've stepped back from all the details to think about what we've learned. More than anything else, we realize that what separates the successful from the unsuccessful is the ability to build trusting, purposeful, mutually beneficial relationships. Of course, like you, we've always known that relationships are important in business. What we hadn't appreciated is that in addition to requiring a lot of hard work, successful collaborative relationships require an analytical and disciplined approach.

Like many things in life, some people have an in-born, intuitive ability to build trusting, win-win relationships both in business and in their personal life. However, for the majority of us, this ability isn't programmed into our DNA. For us, the ability to build trusting relationships requires understanding and practice. With understanding and practice, we, too, can develop this ability.

And that's fortunate because now, more than ever, we need to work collaboratively to better understand our customers' changing needs and take aggressive action to profitably meet those needs. Indeed, the necessity to work across traditional boundaries with like-minded people to achieve shared goals and the benefit from doing so have never been greater. But how do you truly evaluate which relationships are the right relationships to develop and nurture?

This book identifies and describes how you build, measure, and manage successful collaborative relationships. We call this skill *Purposeful Collaboration* and have methodically spelled out the step-by-step process it follows. Further, we have used the detailed description of that process to develop several analog and digital tools that, when coupled with your growing understanding, empower you to successfully build and maintain collaborative relationships.

Once you have developed the ability to trade in relationship currencies, you can focus your limited resources on those relationships that provide you the greatest benefit and offer the fastest return. Very simply, it's how you do business in the era of collaborative business.

PART ONE

The Era of
Collaborative Business

CHAPTER 1

The Collaboration Imperative

▮ **Tuesday, September 11, 2001,** started out like any other summer day. But by day's end, the world as we knew it had changed. Forever.

We are living in volatile times. Uncertainty reigns. Business patterns are changing as the result of social, political, economic, and technological developments. Most tragically, recent global events have complicated the business landscape in ways we have yet to fully understand.

Even before the terrorist attacks of September 11, 2001, the global economy was undergoing a transformation felt through consolidations and downsizings. Now we are in a phase, at least for the foreseeable future, in which conservation of resources is the order of the day. It seems that everything that was true about business no longer holds.

Why? Because of two fundamental truths of the networked economy:

1. *The power in business relationships has shifted to customers. As a result . . .*

2. *Traditional business and industry structures are dying.*

Not all businesspeople have equated these two major developments with declining sales, plummeting valuations, and soaring layoffs. Others have a sense of the association and are trying to see their way clear. Not *all* of the economic malaise of the years 2000 to 2002 is due to these two developments, or factors; some of it is certainly due to the uncertainty elevated by the attacks of September 11. However, it would be a mistake to disregard the profound impact these two factors have had. Think about it. Why should the business and industry structures that worked during the business-centric era be expected to work now that we are in the customer-centric era? They shouldn't and they don't.

But all is not bleak. The economic transformation caused by the ongoing shift from product-centric to customer-centric business models resulting from rapid changes in communication and information technologies may, in fact, turn out to be our trump card. This shift in the balance of power in business relationships to customers has led us to a new business paradigm that is developing across industries, embracing both customers and business partners. It is the era of collaborative business, where commerce is done in trading communities (what we call Collaborative Communities) built by creating win-win relationships with customers and business partners through a continuous stream of value propositions that help each party achieve its respective goals.

▌ In the era of collaborative business, commerce is conducted in trading communities built by creating win-win relationships with customers and business partners.

When business is practiced in trading communities, it changes everything about how business gets done. Every aspect of business is impacted—from what constitutes a business entity and the products and services it offers to the jobs we perform each day and how we produce value and improve company performance. And most assuredly, the attacks of September 11 crystallized the complex interdependencies that exist between companies and nations and further demonstrated the necessity to work with like-minded people to achieve shared goals and the benefit from doing so.

THE NEED TO COLLABORATE

It is the new business mantra—*collaborate, collaborate, collaborate.* But what is collaboration and why is everyone talking about it?

Collaboration has many meanings, depending with whom you speak. Some call collaboration the ability to work with others in distant locations just as you would if they were physically across the table in the same room. For others, collaboration is about the free flow of information across boundaries. And for still others, it is the sharing of resources and goals.

More precisely, *Merriam Webster's Collegiate Dictionary* (10th ed.) defines collaboration as "(1) working jointly with others with whom one is not immediately connected and (2) cooperating with, or willingly assisting, an enemy of one's country." What's interesting is that during World War I and World War II, the word *collaboration* took on a sinister meaning. It was used almost exclusively as cooperating with the enemy, and no one wanted to be accused of being a collaborator. But that was then. Today, collaboration is used more positively. Both in business and in war, collaboration is viewed as essential for success.

Collaboration is considered vital because companies and nations realize that they can no longer go it alone. To survive in the networked economy where the balance of power has shifted to the customer, companies are learning that they *must* collaborate with their customers and other businesses in the design, development, and delivery of the market basket of goods and services if they expect to profitably satisfy their customers' personal needs.

Listen to how Bob Evans, editor-in-chief of *InformationWeek*, a trade publication that made collaborative business an editorial focus, describes the importance of collaboration in business:

> The 21st century will force companies of all stripes to collaborate aggressively and religiously, both inside the company and outwardly with its partners. . . . More than ever before, the intertwined worlds of business and technology will wrap into one unified thread: business goals and objectives outlined and defined by all parties, metrics and milestones determined in partnership, stewardship of various projects taken up by the appropriate leaders . . . The issue—the reality—is collaboration. (Reprinted with permission of *Information-Week*, CMP Media, Manhasset, NY)

Likewise, nations now realize that they *must* collaborate with the people of other nations to survive and prosper. British Prime Minister Tony Blair's speech to the Labour Party conference following the September 11 attacks couldn't have argued more eloquently for collaboration: "Our self-interest and our mutual interests are today inextricably woven together."

From our point of view, we see that building the coalition to fight terrorism resembles the new business paradigm. As U.S. President George Bush stated in an October 11, 2001, press conference: "The attack took place on American soil, but it was an attack on the heart and soul of the civilized world. And the world has come together to fight a new and different war."

From this global perspective, the United States assumes the role of what we call the "choreographer," the entity that sees the vision and works to bring order and direction to the movements of the community members, in this case the people and nations of the world who stand opposed to terrorism.

Whether in business or in geopolitics, the choreographer's role is to build relationships by identifying value propositions that could exist between and among the parties based on what each party brings to the relationship. In building this collaboration, the U.S. has structured value propositions with countries such as Pakistan that previously supported the Taliban. Fearing instability, Pakistan offered information about, and access to, the Taliban and Afghanistan to the United States. In return, the United States offered to lift previously ordered economic sanctions (imposed because of the testing of nuclear weapons), and Pakistan's leaders hope that the lifting of sanctions will promote prosperity and political stability by easing the hardships of the Pakistani people.

> ■ **The choreographer's role is to** build relationships by identifying value propositions that could exist between and among the parties.

Certainly, value propositions between nations are fluid and have always iterated as each nation learns more about how the other can help it achieve its goals. In essence, what this Collaborative Community of nations is doing is trading cash and non-cash currencies so that each country moves closer toward meeting its individual goals. At the same time, the Collaborative Community moves closer to meeting its shared goal of rooting out terrorism.

How do we even begin to comprehend what these events will mean for us as individuals and in the way we go about doing our jobs? What will it mean for our families, our companies, our customers, and our business partners? Where it will all lead, we must confess we do not know. But we do know that whatever bright future is possible, the way to work toward that goal is through collaboration. Whether we are looking at business or geopolitics, the benefits of, and the necessity for, working across traditional boundaries with like-minded people to achieve shared goals is undeniable.

BUSINESS TRADING COMMUNITIES

In the era of collaborative business, commerce is done in trading communities that embrace both customers and business partners in trusting, purposeful, win-win relationships. Or stated differently, a Collaborative Community is a seamless alliance of trading partners and customers where everyone benefits by focusing on profitably satisfying the set of needs and wants of the customers who define the community. It is important to understand that regardless of whether these trading partners and the competencies they bring to the community are found in a division of General Electric or in an individual free agent, each entity has to gain value from its participation in the overall business structure, that is, in the community. In other words, each of these entities must believe that the benefits of collaboration exceed the cost of membership. Each entity must see a clear value proposition, just as each customer sees a clear value proposition in a traditional customer–business relationship. In the era of collaborative business, every relationship must be thought of as a customer relationship.

A Collaborative Community focuses on satisfying the needs and wants of each customer on an increasingly personalized basis. Thus it requires the entity that builds the community to have as its core competency the ability to develop a relationship with, and understand the needs of, the customer. This member must also build the alliance of business partners that provide the additional competencies required to profitably satisfy the customer. This member is the choreographer, as noted before in the example of the United States–led coalition against terrorism; the choreographer is the entity that sees the vision for the community and works to bring order and direction to the movements of the members in pursuit of their shared goals. And just as we call this role player the choreographer, we call the give and take of information, access, goods, services, and money between and among the trading partners and the customers the "dance."

Of course, one can say this dance with customers and businesses has always gone on. And certainly this is true. However, what is different today are the profound developments in information and communication technologies that are transforming the relationships between and among businesses and their customers into Collaborative Communities. As Peter Drucker said at the Collaborative Commerce Summit in June 2001, "The greatest impact of the Internet is the elimination of distance." More than ever, new technologies are allowing people at whatever distance to work closer together. And it is these new information and communication technologies that require us as businesspeople to adopt new perspectives and master new communication and relationship skills.

■ **New information and communication technologies** require new perspectives and new communication and relationship skills.

EVERYONE IS A CUSTOMER

As companies today realize that to profitably satisfy their customers' needs, they must focus on what they do best and collaborate with both their customers and other business entities in order to provide a complete solution, they are also realizing that all parties involved must receive something *they* value for the collaboration to work effectively. And if every party must receive something of value, then by definition *everyone is a customer.*

When you look at business relationships from the perspective that each party in a relationship is a customer, the way to develop these relationships becomes more obvious. "If you are willing to help me achieve my goals, then I'm willing to help you achieve your goals." Of course.

In a business setting, we interact with other entities (individuals or businesses) to learn and make better assumptions about the set of needs and wants we're trying to satisfy and how to build a profitable business around satisfying that set of needs and wants. This is the iterative process of building a business, developing relationships one interaction at a time.

In iterative relationships (and all relationships are iterative), each relationship starts with an assumption about the needs and wants the relationship is trying to satisfy and how the relationship should go about satisfying them. Then, in the actual process of conducting the relationship, the assumptions are tested against reality. If the relationship is to endure, whatever works must be kept; whatever is found lacking must be adjusted and improved. This pattern is how all relationships are developed, one interaction at a time.

While everyone experiences this pattern, understanding it allows one to shape it, grow it, feel it, and, in business, profit from it! The iterative process of moving a business forward one step at a time helps you know how to (1) get and keep customers, (2) develop the products and services that satisfy customers' needs, and (3) deliver to, and service, customers. This organic, iterative process is in stark contrast to the traditional win-lose, zero-sum game that is the conventional thinking about how business is transacted. Unfortunately, this organic, iterative process, while practiced intuitively by successful entrepreneurs, has largely gone unnoticed by business thinkers, writers, and practitioners. In fact, conventional thinking has so dominated business that it is fairly common to find companies devoting resources to overlapping product lines that compete against one another in order to please the same customer, thus dissipating their critical resources without a clear gain.

Today's efficient businesses should use an iterative approach to discovering and satisfying the needs and wants of their customers. And today the term *customer* not only means the traditional customer but every entity that interacts with you in a significant manner.

Of course, "The customer is in control," "Whatever the customer wants," or "The customer is king" are slogans that supposedly have guided business thinking for years. Whenever we hear companies espousing these platitudes, we think of one of the favorite expressions of Guy Kawasaki, founder and CEO of Garage Technology Ventures (formerly called Garage.com) and former chief evangelist of Apple Computer: "There's marketing and then there's the truth."

Yes, it is true that any progressive company's marketing messages trumpet its customer focus. Some individuals even believe their company's propaganda. But too few businesses actually infuse that sentiment into their culture and operations. Despite talk of making the "demand chain" the driver of value, businesspeople by and large don't understand how to profitably deliver what their customers want. Think about all the companies that render an inconsistent customer experience across different touch points, provide abominable customer service, and waste limited resources developing products and services no one wants.

Many of the companies we as consumers deal with on a daily basis are the worst offenders in all three areas. Consider telecommunications providers, insurance companies, banks, airlines, and even the local retail establishments we frequent—from the dry cleaner who after ten visits still asks us how we want our shirts to our favorite take-out restaurant that still asks our phone number even though the staff recognizes our voice and all-too-predictable order. The result: Sales don't close; hard-won and expensive-to-acquire customers are lost; and unsold inventories mount. What it all means is that business assets aren't providing the return on investment they should—in other words, money is left on the table.

Yet if we asked the heads of the companies we deal with daily about their customer focus, they would proclaim with absolute sincerity, "The customer is king!" Such hypocrisy simply can't continue in a world where the balance of power has shifted to customers. To achieve and maintain success in a customer-centric environment, you *must* look at all your business relationships as if they were customers and from their perspective.

> ▌ **You *must* look at all** your business relationships as if they were customers and from their perspective.

Let's take a closer look at what we mean by the term *perspective*. According to *Webster's Dictionary*, perspective is "a point of view . . . i.e., the capacity to view things in their true relations or relative importance." And that's exactly right. Until you sit in the customer's chair, you will not see things in their true relative importance. However, once you view things from a customer's perspective, you have the ability to reexamine all of your business relationships and see where each party perceives a possible exchange of goods, services, access, information, and money that is of value to each.

By viewing everyone as a customer, (1) you fundamentally change the nature of the value proposition that exists between you and the entities with whom you interact; (2) you recognize that value can be realized through cash as well as through the exchange of "currencies" other than cash; and (3) you are able to make better assumptions about your business as a result of the frequency of interactions and depth of information you must build and maintain in your efforts to form successful collaborative relationships.

The value creation process in the era of collaborative business begins and ends with knowledgeable and powerful customers who require satisfaction of their personal needs. Therefore, throughout your business every relationship must be viewed as a customer relationship. It is up to you to develop these relationships and monetize them.

IT'S ALL ABOUT RELATIONSHIPS

Truly collaborative relationships require knowledge that builds and sustains the relationships by delivering on promises. Yet as collaborative business becomes more and more the imperative, companies are having an extremely difficult time making collaboration successful over the long term. Conventional wisdom holds that most alliances fail. Research by Accenture <www.accenture.com> supports that perception by finding that 30 percent of alliances fail completely and another 49 percent fail to meet expectations. Whether referred to as outsourcing arrangements, joint marketing agreements, distribution partnerships, or industry consortia, alliances have become the norm. However, what isn't understood is the reason these alliances fail. It isn't financial; it is because of breakdowns in the relationships between the participants.

Does this mean that although collaboration works in theory, it can't be practically applied? Not at all. But the question does strike at the heart of the problem, which is that relationships are advertised as being between companies, whereas in reality relationships are built between people. And that's a very important distinction.

Relationships by definition are always between the individual people who interact. Companies interact only as the result of the actions people take on their behalf. A company's relationship with another company is really the sum of the individual relationships between and among the people in the different companies. So, in essence, in order to determine if your collaborative efforts are achieving their desired results, you must summarize all of the individual relationships and determine if, in fact, they do add up to the intended relationship between the two companies.

❚ **Relationships by definition are** always between the individual people who interact.

And that's when the problems begin—in the building of all those nitty-gritty working relationships that in theory, at least, are supposed to lead to the intended outcomes between two companies. The seriousness of this problem is underscored by a May 21, 2001, *Forbes.com* article: "[T]he winners in this new age of partnering will be those companies that attract others and are skilled at managing the relationships."

So how do you do it? How do you look at the myriad relationships that your company has, or rather that you and your colleagues have, and evaluate whether they are adding value?

Because the foundation of collaborative business lies not in the technical tools for communication and information processing but in the underlying human relationships that are ultimately responsible for the activities that take place within the collaboration, collaborative business is not easily quantified and controlled. This lack of analytical mechanisms puts collaborative relationships at risk.

■ **The lack of analytical mechanisms** puts collaborative relationships at risk.

Observing this problem, we developed an iterative methodology for effectively analyzing *both* how to decide with what individuals and companies to form collaborative relationships and then how to make the underlying business relationships work. Using this iterative methodology, you can correctly evaluate which relationships provide the greatest value and allocate the proper resources to those relationships, thereby improving your performance and increasing your profits.

WHAT HAVE WE LEARNED?

1 ∎ Business patterns are changing as the result of social, political, economic, and technological developments.

2 ∎ Two fundamental truths of the networked economy: (1) *The power in business relationships has shifted to customers.* As a result ... (2) *Traditional business and industry structures are dying.*

3 ∎ It is the era of collaborative business, where commerce is conducted in trading communities (what we call Collaborative Communities) built by creating win-win relationships with customers and business partners through a continuous stream of value propositions that helps each party achieve its respective goals.

4 ∎ When business is practiced in trading communities, it changes everything about how business gets done.

5 ∎ To survive in the networked economy, where the balance of power has shifted to the customer, companies are learning that they *must* collaborate with their customers and other businesses in the design, development, and delivery of a market basket of goods and services if they expect to profitably satisfy their customers' personal needs.

6 ∎ The choreographer's role is to build relationships by identifying value propositions that could exist between and among the parties based on what each party brings to the relationship.

7 ∎ Whether we are looking at business or geopolitics, the benefits of, and the necessity for, working across traditional boundaries with like-minded people to achieve shared goals is undeniable.

8 ∎ A Collaborative Community is a seamless alliance of trading partners and customers where everyone benefits by focusing on profitably satisfying the set of needs and wants of the customers who define the community.

9 ∎ A Collaborative Community requires the entity that builds the community to have as its core competency the ability to develop a relationship with, and understand the needs of, the customer.

10 ∎ New information and communication technologies require us as businesspeople to adopt new perspectives and master new communication and relationship skills.

11 ∎ For collaboration to work effectively, all parties involved must receive something *they* value. And if every party must receive something of value, then by definition *everyone is a customer.*

12 ∎ The iterative process of moving a business forward one step at a time helps you know how to (1) get and keep customers, (2) develop the products and services that satisfy customers' needs, and (3) deliver to and service customers.

13 ∎ By viewing everyone as a customer you (1) fundamentally change the nature of the value proposition that exists between you and the entities with whom you interact; (2) recognize that value can be realized through cash as well as through the exchange of "currencies" other than cash; and (3) realize this perspective allows you to make better assumptions about your business.

14 ∎ Relationships by definition are always between the individual people who interact. Companies only interact as the result of the actions people take on their behalf.

15 ∎ The foundation of collaborative business lies not in the technical tools for communication and information processing but in the un-

derlying human relationships that are ultimately responsible for the activities that take place within the collaboration.

16 ▐ Because collaborative business is relationship based as opposed to transaction based, it is not easily quantified and controlled. This lack of analytical mechanisms puts collaborative relationships at risk.

CHAPTER 2

Collaborative Communities

Because of the shift in power to customers, we are in the era of collaborative business. Collaborative business is conducted within networks of relationships more appropriately referred to as trading communities. Whether they are described as living organisms, business webs, value nets, value webs, or our choice, Collaborative Communities, these business-trading communities are the models for value creation as we leave product-centric, company-focused business models behind.

What differentiates a Collaborative Community from other new models is that in a Collaborative Community every member benefits from its focus on the end consumers' needs or business problem around which a choreographer organizes the community. Thus, a choreographer structures a Collaborative Community into trusting, purposeful, mutually beneficial relationships with both its consumers and business partners. Consumers (whether individuals or businesses) are the end customers for any community's principal products and services, while business partners provide the competencies required to satisfy the consumers. But in a Collaborative Community, value is exchanged between and among all business relationships so that everyone is viewed as a customer.

SHARED NEEDS

Before we look at some Collaborative Communities, it is important to understand why we focus on the end, or principal, customers' needs and not on customer profiles.

Customer profiles are ingrained as a marketing tool, and companies have grown comfortable focusing on customer-based demographic and behavioral profiling variables. However, given today's knowledgeable and powerful customers, who increasingly require satisfaction of their personal needs, it no longer makes sense to limit the understanding of customers to their profile, no matter how narrowly defined. The variety, the individuality is too significant. What assumes primary importance is not who the customer is in terms of age or income or size of company but rather the set of needs and wants that customer has.

This difference is extremely important. We focus on the set of needs and wants rather than on the customer profile because we are making decisions from the customer's viewpoint, *not* the business's. Looking at your customers from your business's point of view always produces a gap in understanding and thus leaves money on the table. Looking at your business from the customer's perspective naturally narrows the gap and puts money in your pocket. Our viewpoint therefore raises the following questions: How do we define a set of needs and wants? How does focusing on this set of needs and wants allow us to make decisions from the customer's viewpoint? And how does this focus make a difference in the design and operation of a business?

As individuals, all of us have thousands of needs and wants, ranging from the essentials of life, such as safety and security, to seemingly frivolous needs, such as the latest music recordings. Companies, too, have many needs that follow a similar pattern, as companies are but fluid collections of people organized for a specific profit-making purpose. From the customer's perspective, we generally deal with these needs and wants by grouping them into sets. We think of them in terms of interest areas and experiences. For example, a house-buying experience consists of interactions with real estate agents, insurance agents, mortgage brokers, and various tradespeople. Or our strong interest in football results in interactions with football teams and stadiums, cable TV, magazines, newspapers, and memorabilia stores. Thus, for businesses it makes sense to group their customers' needs and wants into sets of shared patterns and concerns related to these shared experiences.

How broadly or narrowly do we define the set of needs and wants?

Generally speaking, the set of needs and wants has to be narrow enough so customers can opt into what becomes a group. Yet it must be broad enough so that both the choreographer (the builder of the community) and its business partners can make an acceptable profit. In other words, depending on the price of your products and services and the profit margins your company makes with each sale, you must define the set of needs and wants to encompass a group of sufficient size to keep your company financially healthy.

Once we have defined the set of customers' needs and wants, it is best to think of the customers who have this shared interest as a self-identifying virtual community. Its members could cover the world or be located in one geographical area. They could work within a single industry or across multiple industries. The salient feature of each community is its specific set of needs and wants. The community does not have to literally come together at any time, although that is entirely possible. These virtual communities thus represent unprecedented opportunities for companies to make the products and services required to precisely satisfy their customers by collaborating with them toward the fulfillment of an entire category of their needs. For example, customers of a bicycle manufacturer have shared interests around the product itself—maintaining it, accessorizing it, utilizing it most effectively—that the company could support, thereby extending its relationship with the customers. The company could also provide customers with information about races, biking clubs, and the hottest new biking fashions.

WineAccess <www.wineaccess.com> based in Narberth, Pennsylvania, has positioned itself as the largest online wine-shopping community. In the founder's message on the company's Web site <www.wineaccess.com/static/word-from-founder.tcl>, Jim Weinrott says:

> After 16 years in the wine industry, I decided to bring Main Street (where merchants knew their customers and their needs) to the Web, to use technology to allow buyers and sellers to come together in a new kind of shopping community. First we help buyers find the best local merchants. Then we automate the buying process by allowing the buyer to access lots of other recommendations and opinions from other members of the community so as to further refine buying decisions.

The important point is that the customers' set of needs and wants (knowledge of, and access to, the best wines in the world) defines the community as opposed to a profile of who the individuals are. Statistically, the age or income or address of the customers might mean they have a higher or lower probability of buying wine or indicate what type of wine they might want to buy, but a probability is full of hits and misses and provides no real personal connection.

On the other hand, customers who comprise a Collaborative Community are similar because of a shared interest they desire to have satisfied. All are hits and the connection is personal.

(Every member of WineAccess is a wine lover.) Individuals or companies never comprise a Collaborative Community just because they fit a particular customer profile.

> ▮ **The choreographer translates knowledge** of the customers' needs into trusting, profitable, win-win relationships with its business partners.

THE NEW BUSINESS PATTERN

As shown in Figure 2.1, a Collaborative Community is made up of three major constituencies: (1) knowledgeable and powerful customers who selectively share information about themselves in order to have their own needs satisfied one at a time on a personal

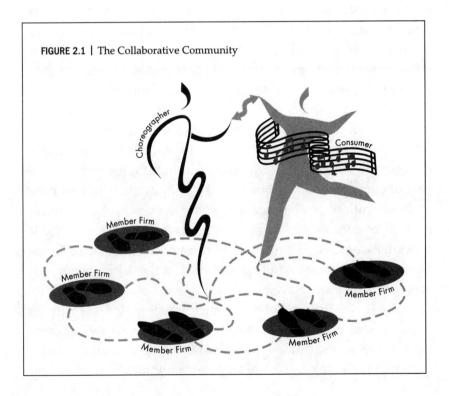

FIGURE 2.1 | The Collaborative Community

basis; (2) member firms/business partners (suppliers, distributors, and those providing support functions); and (3) the choreographer. As the builder of the community, the choreographer has
the role of understanding customers' needs and earning their trust
and then translating that knowledge and trust into profitable,
win-win relationships with its business partners.

As we said, the totality of any given customer's sets of needs
and wants is defined from the customer's perspective by interest
areas or experiences. Because Collaborative Communities are organized around a specific set of customer needs and wants, every
customer is therefore a member of many communities. And as
customers' needs and wants change over time and customers develop new sets of needs and wants, a customer can be thought of
as continuously opting into and out of many communities. In the
same way, both the choreographer and its business partners also
belong to many communities at any given time and take on different roles in those communities. In one community a business
may be a supplier. In another it may be a customer. And just as
customers opt into and out of communities, businesses will themselves opt into and out of communities as customer needs change
and new technologies are developed and introduced.

Further, any business will have various networks of companies that it will work with in producing its different product
offerings. So we can look at the world as an interlaced, interchanging network of self-identifying communities both on the
part of customers and businesses. The implications of this type
of collaboration are significant. A company can no longer think
of itself as competing with another company for customers. It
must think of itself as a member of multiple Collaborative Communities of businesses and customers and think of its competitors in this manner as well.

The stronger the relationship the choreographer has with its
customers, the better it can understand their needs and provide
the knowledge its business partners require to assist the choreographer in meeting those needs. The result: more satisfied cus-

tomers and more profitable businesses. Remember that businesses participate in a community only if they see clear and profitable value propositions.

In essence, the Collaborative Community affords each business member transparent access to the specific information it requires, from product design to product delivery. Of significance, this flow of information throughout the Collaborative Community also allows the end customer transparent access, from product design to product delivery, thus giving the customer the means to provide input back to the business members on how best to satisfy his or her needs on a personalized basis.

> ▌ **The Collaborative Community affords each** business member and each customer transparent access to the specific information each requires.

In addition, this multiple community participation provides its participants the opportunity to share information across the various communities to which they belong (as long as they don't violate trust and confidentiality agreements). The accrual of this shared information is a valuable asset to every member of the community and in most instances enhances each business's ability to operate successfully in all of its other communities.

As the needs and wants of customers change, the composition of the Collaborative Community itself must change, and the way each business in the community operates must change. The goal, of course, is to change in a manner that continually leads to an increased ability of the community to profitably satisfy customers.

THE CHOREOGRAPHER

Let's take a closer look at the role of the choreographer, whom you can think of as the *entrepreneur* of the Collaborative

Community. The choreographer is the entity that builds the business and information infrastructure around the set of customer needs and wants.

We call the leader of the Collaborative Community a choreographer because the skills required to accomplish the goals of the Collaborative Community are similar to those required of a choreographer of dance. *Encyclopaedia Britannica* describes choreography as "the gathering and organization of movement into order and pattern. The choreographic process may be divided for analytical purposes (the divisions are never distinct in practice) into three phases: gathering together the movement material, developing movements into dance phrases, and creating the final structure of the work."

So we use the metaphor the *choreographer* because just as a choreographer in a musical must select different dancers for different roles, ensure that all of the dancers follow the same rhythm, and encourage every dancer to work together to accomplish the same goal, the choreographer of the Collaborative Community assembles all of the businesses required to satisfy a set of needs and wants, arranges that these businesses function in coordination and synchrony, and motivates each and every business to work together to accomplish their goals profitably.

Clearly, the choreographer's position within the Collaborative Community is one of great value. Listen to how Mohanbir Sawhney and Deval Parikh, writing in the January 2001 *Harvard Business Review,* describe the role: "Much of the competition in the business world will center on gaining and maintaining the orchestration role for a value chain or industry. . . . More money can be made in managing interactions than in performing actions."

The implications of this shift to Collaborative Communities are profound. To get a better feel for how choreographers are building Collaborative Communities around shared interests and shaping their business model from the customer's perspective, let's take a look at some examples.

LET'S MEET SOME CHOREOGRAPHERS

When we think about industries today, we see that they are defined from the business's perspective, not the customer's. Thus, we tend to think of business in a product or service orientation. We think about the movie industry, the clothing industry, the automobile industry, the oil industry, and so on—what the industry does and how it does it. However, from a customer's perspective, it's never about which industry you're in or what products you make; it's only about the satisfaction of customer needs and wants or, more specifically, the satisfaction of a set of customer needs and wants as defined by an interest area or a buying experience. How does this perspective change how we look at business?

Let's look again at our example of home ownership. When buying and occupying a new home, we think of our needs as finding the home, negotiating the deal, arranging the financing, obtaining insurance, selling our existing home, moving, establishing new utility connections, renovating and remodeling, and so forth. Yet companies tend to divide these needs and wants into separate and disconnected industries. In this example, despite the fact that all of the services described are related to the experience of one customer selling one home and occupying another, often the customer has to establish and engage in relationships with many different businesses in many different industries—real estate, finance, insurance, and so forth—to satisfy one home ownership experience.

Therefore, we can see that if we structure a business from the customer's point of view, we get an entirely different business. From the customer's point of view, we may have a business that encompasses real estate, finance, moving, storage, decorating, and so forth. From the point of view of the business, we get what existed when businesses held the power in the relationship —different industries providing products and services that customers have to deal with simultaneously or in sequence. Building your business from the customer's perspective costs less in the aggregate because of the savings from eliminating redundant operations. Customers get what they want and businesses working collaboratively are more profitable.

Not surprisingly, the real estate industry is one of the first to adopt collaborative business models. Let's look at a couple of companies in the residential real estate business that understand the new reality, although they are implementing their understanding differently. The companies are Hometouch Centers <www.hometouch.com> based in Chicago, Illinois, and the DeWolfe Companies <www.dewolfe.com> of Lexington, Massachusetts.

If you are a customer selling a home, traditionally you deal with a real estate company briefly. It finds you a buyer, and you pay it a commission but never see it again. But Hometouch and DeWolfe understand that homesellers are also homebuyers who have a much broader set of needs. Thus, they define their primary customer as a homebuyer.

For example, Hometouch claims to have been created to fill the needs of current and future homeowners. The company is opening stores in shopping malls to make it more convenient for consumers to come to them and, through the use of technology, is providing innovative services and easy access to information. Every consumer works with a team of professionals to help "find, buy, enhance, and manage" the home ownership experience. To satisfy the consumer's complete set of home ownership needs, Hometouch offers such services, among others, as locating a home, having it inspected, finding the right mortgage, getting the home properly insured, and moving. The company also helps homeowners improve and repair their home through a network of vetted contractors and home service specialists. And the service doesn't end there. Hometouch consumers are able to store documents and keep track of maintenance records, warranties, and other information related to the home ownership experience through Hometouch's Web site.

This type of relationship between a real estate company and the customer arises from looking at the home-buying process from the viewpoint of the consumer. It doesn't end at the closing of the deal when you get either the check or the keys. Buying a home creates long-term needs and Hometouch is positioning itself to continue profiting from those needs. By creating a community of vendors that can service homeowners, it is fulfilling the needs of the homeowners with low-cost, high-quality goods and services. And the company is fulfilling the needs of the community of vendors with inexpensive access to new customers; it is fulfilling its own needs with a continuous stream of income from customers who in traditional industry thinking would already be forgotten.

Hometouch is a relatively new business led by Gary Rosenberg, an entrepreneur with many years of experience in the real estate industry. DeWolfe, on the other hand, is a publicly traded company with $6 billion in sales and has been in business for more than 50 years. The company has been expanding the set of customer needs it intends to satisfy since 1976 when it launched its relocation services. In 1997, it began to promote its services as one-stop shopping, claiming to simplify the home ownership process. The company offers its customers "everything essential to buy or sell your home"; it offers "buying and selling services, mortgages, insurance, relocation and moving management, as well as a number of expanding e-services" <www.dewolfe.com>. Thus, DeWolfe does not provide all services essential to the home ownership experience as defined by Hometouch. However, DeWolfe clearly understands that the greater the number of home-related transactions it is involved in, the greater its share of a customer's home ownership dollar.

DeWolfe also has different financial relationships with the businesses in its community than does Hometouch. In many instances, DeWolfe has expanded its complement of product and service offerings through acquisition, thus making that particular product or service part of the company's core competencies.

Hometouch, on the other hand, represents its core competencies as its role as the buyer's representative and its partnering with companies that have complementary competencies. Both types of relationships can be equally rewarding. However, a relationship strategy that focuses the core competencies of a company on a specific and well-defined customer need is more flexible and thus better able to iterate as customers and their needs change.

Here is another example. This one demonstrates how technology is enabling a truly traditional business to reach a broader group of customers with a shared set of needs when previously it had narrowed its customer base because it was too expensive for the business to reach the entire community of need. Milpro.com <www.milpro.com> is a Web site operated by $1 billion machine tool manufacturer Milacron, which began in the mid-1860s as a small machine shop in downtown Cincinnati. The company's Web site sells coolants, cutting wheels, and drill bits to small machine shops. These customers, difficult and expensive to reach through traditional channels, are using self-service features on the Web site to diagnose problems, address business challenges, buy and sell used equipment, and collaboratively solve problems with other customers. The value proposition is clear: the machine shops gain access to otherwise unaffordable expertise and Milacron gets a profitable customer.

Regardless of how long you've been in business, no matter how many customers you have, or how large your company's revenues and profits are, you can and should embrace the Collaborative Community as the business pattern for achieving success in the era of collaborative business. Collaboration stems from abandoning legacy thinking and looking at business from the perspective of the customer and figuring out how to create a community of businesses and customers that interact with each other in a mutually beneficial and personal manner.

As we've said, traditional industry structures are vestiges of another era that are in the process of dying.

MINDSET OF AN ENTREPRENEUR, SKILLSET OF A CHOREOGRAPHER

In Chapter 1's description of a Collaborative Community, we said that it was a seamless alliance of competencies needed to satisfy a set of customers' needs. We also stated that these competencies can be found essentially anywhere—in a division of General Electric or in an individual free agent. But what is a free agent?

Since his article "Free Agent Nation" first appeared in *Fast Company* in January 1998, Daniel Pink has been chronicling the development of this new workforce trend:

> In the second half of the twentieth century, the key to understanding America's social and economic life was the Organization man. In the first half of the twenty-first century, the new emblematic figure is the free agent—the independent worker who operates on his or her own terms, untethered to a large organization, serving multiple clients and customers instead of a single boss.

What's interesting is that in the three years between the time the article appeared and the publication of Dan's book *Free Agent Nation*, the number of free agents has grown from approximately 25 million to more than 33 million individuals. According to Dan, free agents usually represent three general species: soloists (16.5 million), temps (3.5 million), and micro-businesses (13 million), which means there are 33 million free agents—or about one in four American workers.

We'll go one step further than Dan. It is our view that today, unlike ever before, *everyone* must view himself or herself as a free agent. That's right. Everyone!

Listen to how Michael Schrage, codirector of the Massachusetts Institute of Technology's Media Lab's e-markets initiative, characterizes the profound change that has taken place in today's workplace:

> Bursting bubbles and toppling towers have utterly destroyed the cheery truism that "people are a company's most important resource."
>
> The truth is that the perception of viability is what matters most. If uncertainty exceeds opportunity, companies become loyal to their own survival. Tsunami after tsunami of layoffs affirms the darkest of managerial suspicions: When the going gets tough, the tough send out pink slips. We knew it all along. We are all contingency workers now. (*Fortune,* 12 Nov. 2001)

We couldn't agree more. In today's volatile and uncertain business environment, every businessperson, whether currently employed as a C-level executive, middle manager, or individual contributor, has to view herself or himself as a business of one, a contingency worker . . . a free agent.

Furthermore, as Dan Pink sees it, even corporations appreciate the skillset and mindset of free agents. Says Dan:

> More and more people are going to hold dual passports—one in Corporate America, one in Free Agent Nation. And they'll be able to migrate between those two places fairly easily. Today, I've found in talking with line managers and some human resource people that they love to hire people who have worked for themselves. Why? Those people don't need any handholding. They don't expect to be with the organization for twenty years. And they have proven themselves out in the marketplace. Somebody who's succeeded on her own for a few years is probably pretty good at what she does. Instead of it being a barrier to getting a job in corporate America, self-employment can actu-

ally be a boon. So you're going to have people who will be able to go back and forth relatively easily between free agency and traditional employment. It won't be a big deal. But it will deeply affect corporate America. So the companies that don't start treating people like free agents will end up without decent talent. Inevitably they're going to be pressured to treat people like free agents. And that means the border between who is a free agent and who is not is going to get muddier.

Although the concept of a free agent covers many different individual work-life profiles, *every* free agent *must* understand and adopt the mindset of an entrepreneur. We believe that the entrepreneurial mindset required for achieving and maintaining success is rooted in what we call the four building blocks of business: process, customers, information, and timing:

1. **Process.** Most simply, the process is iterative. Iterative processes can be applied to different areas, such as building relationships, projects, or business models, but they always consist of four steps: (1) assumptions, (2) preparation/testing, (3) learning, and (4) refining/new assumptions. When building a business, the four steps are making assumptions about how to develop a business model that satisfies your customers' needs and wants, developing and testing the business model in the marketplace, learning from that test, and then refining the results and creating new assumptions about how your business model can more accurately and profitably fulfill your customers' needs and wants. And remember that this process of iteration is continual. It never stops.

2. **Customers.** Business is not about beating the competition; it's about satisfying the customer. And now you

must view everyone as a customer as well as view your business from the perspective of the customer.

3. **Information.** The value of information appears when you gather, process, and connect it. Connecting the information is like the game of "Connect the Dots." When you connect the dots, you see a picture. When you connect the information, you see a pattern. The fewer the pieces of information you need to connect to see the pattern, the more quickly you can act. This requires you to get the right information to the right person at the right time.

4. **Timing.** The length of time it takes to decide that an assumption is valid or is in need of change is directly related to how much information you gather and how quickly you can process and connect it, and is therefore a measure of your sense of timing (knowing the exact moment when to take action). Your ability to process and connect information in turn is based on your talent, your experience, and your dedication to your business. Your talent, your experience, your dedication, and your timing together form your intuition.

Further, as Dan Pink points out, a free agent "provides talent (products, services, and advice) in exchange for opportunity (money, learning, and connections)." Essentially, free agents provide their competencies/skills in a collaborative manner to their own ever changing Collaborative Community. And because today everyone is a free agent, you need to view yourself as the choreographer of your own Collaborative Community. Consequently, in addition to having the mindset of an entrepreneur, you must have the skillset of a choreographer. If you are to be successful, there simply is no other option.

❚ **You need to view yourself** as the choreographer of your own Collaborative Community.

You may recall that we ended the preface by describing our challenge as answering a simple, but fundamentally important, question: How do you do business in the era of collaborative business? We now have part of the answer:

▮ Everyone has to have the mindset of an entrepreneur and the skillset of a choreographer.

In the era of collaborative business, business is done in trading communities where everyone is a customer. Everyone has to have the mindset of an entrepreneur and the skillset of a choreographer.

WHAT HAVE WE LEARNED?

1 ▮ In a Collaborative Community every member benefits from its focus on the ultimate consumer need or business problem around which a choreographer organizes the community.

2 ▮ We focus on the set of needs and wants rather than on the customer profile because we are making decisions from the customer's viewpoint, *not* the business's.

3 ▮ The set of needs and wants has to be narrow enough so customers can opt into what becomes a group. Yet it must be broad enough so that both the choreographer and its business partners can make an acceptable profit.

4 ▮ A Collaborative Community is made up of three major constituencies: (1) knowledgeable and powerful customers who selectively share the information businesses need to have their own needs satisfied, one at a time on a personal basis; (2) member firms/business partners (suppliers, distributors, and those providing support functions); and (3) the choreographer.

5 ▮ The choreographer understands the needs, and earns the trust, of customers and then translates that knowledge and trust into profitable, win-win relationships with its business partners.

6 ▮ We can look at the world as an interlaced, interchanging network of self-identifying communities on the part of both customers and businesses.

7 ▮ The Collaborative Community affords each business member and each customer transparent access to the specific information it requires from product design to product delivery.

8 ▮ As the needs and wants of customers change, the composition of the Collaborative Community itself must change, and the way each business in the community operates must change.

9 ▮ In today's volatile and uncertain business environment, every businessperson has to view herself or himself as a business of one, a contingency worker ... a free agent.

10 ▮ *Every* businessperson *must* understand and adopt the mindset of the entrepreneur. We believe that the entrepreneurial mindset required for achieving and maintaining success is rooted in what we call the four building blocks of business: process, customers, information, and timing.

11 ▮ In the era of collaborative business, business is done in trading communities where everyone is a customer. Everyone has to have the mindset of an entrepreneur and the skillset of a choreographer.

CHAPTER 3

Everyone Is a Customer

W e started Chapter 1 by claiming that because of advances in communications and information technologies, the power in business relationships is passing to customers, a shift resulting in the overturning of traditional business and industry structures. In the business and product-centric era we are leaving behind, there were customer relationships, distribution relationships, supplier relationships, and so on. Because it is generally preferable to do business from a position of strength, if the customer is in control, shouldn't everyone in any business relationship now want to be perceived as occupying the position of strength? Thus, our premise is that to achieve and maintain success in today's customer-centric era of collaborative business, *every* relationship must take on the characteristics of a customer relationship. In this way, each party receives something it values. The old adage, "You've got to give in order to get," has never been truer.

HAS THE POWER REALLY SHIFTED TO CUSTOMERS?

Customers have the power because increasingly they can choose with whom they do business and under what terms. Consumers can now configure products and services to their exact liking at a time and in the venue they choose. Customers can do research, gather information, and access goods and services over the Web, yet still want to walk into a conveniently located store and get the same answers and find the same products.

Examples of this ability to personalize our buying experiences abound, from specifying exactly the news that comes to our e-mail in-box to the music we choose one song at a time and on through sneakers of our own design, our personal blend of breakfast cereal, or the home mortgage and credit card exactly suited to our needs.

In a business-to-business setting, this shift of power to customers is often manifested through powerful customers that require suppliers to conform to the customers' way of doing business. Wal-Mart has gained much attention for the specific terms it imposes on suppliers in order to more effectively manage its inventory and thus offer its customers the prices and selection that keep them Wal-Mart's customers. If you want to reach Wal-Mart's customers, you do business on Wal-Mart's terms, or Wal-Mart isn't *your* customer.

As we further expand the automated connections between companies and their powerful customers, these major customers are demanding that suppliers become integrated into their unique supply chain. In essence, the supplier has to do business with the customer in the way each customer sees fit or the customer will find another supplier. According to Dr. David Closs, professor of marketing and logistics at Michigan State University's Eli Broad College of Business, "The supply chain itself is difficult enough, but the technology that each customer is expecting is different as well. If you're selling to Target and Wal-Mart, they're quite different interfaces." And this implies that you increasingly have to look at your business from the perspective of your individual customers and present them with the solution that exactly fits their needs. If you don't provide it, your competitors will.

> ▮ **Look at your business from** the perspective of your customers and present them with the solution that exactly fits their needs.

No doubt you are thinking of instances where you, as a customer, were unable to get what you wanted and thus doubt our point. Of course, this "personalized" vision is not completely true in all instances, but the trend is clearly towards knowledgeable and powerful customers who have access to information and global options. Still, some businesses appear to remain largely beyond customer influence. For example, our experiences with two broadband providers gave us many headaches, so we weren't feeling particularly powerful when we sought yet a third supplier. However, once we did our research and selected a more stable provider, we were heartened as the sales process was relatively smooth and our service fashioned to meet our needs. But that was where our influence ended. Our carrier contracted out the installation to an unsatisfactory and financially unhealthy partner. And that partner refused to honor the terms of the carrier's agreement, leaving us caught in the middle. Fortunately, we are tenacious, and the matter was favorably resolved but not without the significant expenditure of our time.

Does this example disprove that the balance of power has shifted to customers? Not at all. We still had a choice of the type of connection we installed, the speed at which it operates, and whether it was to be integrated with our voice systems. We didn't have to use the vendor we chose, buy the product we bought, or pay the price we paid. We had other options, even though we decided to endure our installer's lack of efficiency and responsibility. The telecommunications industry still has a long way to go in customer service. Although it is advanced technically, its customer perspective is in the Stone Age. But your perspective doesn't have to be.

WHEN EVERYONE'S A CUSTOMER, EVERYONE BENEFITS

Just as you should build your business to satisfy the needs and wants of your primary customers, we also believe that you should look at all your business relationships with a customer focus and examine your business from their perspective. Let's take a look at some of the benefits you realize by adopting the mindset that everyone is a customer.

First, such a mindset fundamentally changes the nature of business relationships. After all, by viewing everyone as a customer, you are in essence looking to develop longer-term, collaborative relationships as opposed to arm's-length, transaction-based relationships. More important, you're developing learning relationships that build trust by continually following through on promises made. In diplomacy, each party needs to develop the trust required to negotiate the issue at hand. As trust is built over time and each party lives up to its commitments, more complex agreements requiring greater sharing of information are negotiated. It is the same in business. Greater knowledge of the companies and individuals you interact with undoubtedly helps you make better and better assumptions about how to balance the two goals of every business: satisfying customers and doing so profitably.

Second, by viewing everyone as a customer you fundamentally change the nature of the value proposition that exists between you and the entities with whom you interact. The value accruing from the bidirectional flow of goods, services, information, access, and money should increase for all concerned. You may even derive revenue where before you saw only costs. For example, your supplier includes you in a how-to brochure the supplier offers to *its* customers because you bring the supplier information about *your* customers that the supplier wants.

■ **Viewing everyone as a customer** fundamentally changes the nature of the value proposition between the entities that interact.

Implicit in changing the value proposition is the recognition and understanding that value can be realized through the exchange of currencies other than cash. *Webster's Dictionary* defines value as "a fair return or equivalent in goods, services, or money for something exchanged, relative worth, utility, or importance." According to generally accepted accounting principles, fair market value is quantified based on the perceived value of that which is given up. And that's the point. Value is determined in the eyes of the beholder. Only the recipient can assess the relative value in something he or she receives. And in many instances non-cash currencies can be of equal or greater utility than cash in achieving certain goals.

■ **Only the recipient can assess** the relative value in something he or she receives. Non-cash currencies can be of equal or greater utility than cash.

What currencies are there other than cash? Most likely you already make use of many of them as you carry out your business, but you might not have thought of them as a currency per se. We include as currencies such valuable resources as (1) access to someone's network of business contacts, (2) use of an important skill, (3) access to someone else's technology, and (4) validation from an important customer of the benefit of your products. By now you are likely writing your own list of what matters to you. For example, Manco, a maker of duct tape and other adhesives, used the non-cash currency of access to a customer's inventory system to better serve that customer when funds for upgrading its own inventory system were not in its budget. Jean V. Murphy, in *Global Logistics & Supply Chain Strategies*, reports this story told by supply chain director Brian Bastock:

> We knew Ace was using a "pretty robust inventory management system. So we approached Ace and asked if there was a way we could dial into their system so that we could all be looking at the same information. . . ." Everyone liked the idea. Ace agreed to set up and maintain firewalls so Manco could see only its inventory positions and forecasts . . . "Today, we dial into their system through the Internet to receive forecast information, resolve exceptions, and plan promotions. It used to be that we would learn about promotions when we got the purchase order, which was often too late to do any really effective cost-conscious planning. Now we are able to get out ahead of that."
>
> In setting up the program the two companies also collaborated on product mix and economic order quantities, taking into consideration logistics and freight costs. By replenishing some products in larger quantities less frequently, Manco was able to save on transportation costs and give Ace a better deal. [Jean V. Murphy, "Forget the 'E'! C-Commerce Is the Next Big Thing," *Global Logistics & Supply Chain Strategies* (August 2001).]

By expanding the value proposition between Manco and Ace to include a non-cash currency, both companies benefited. In essence, Manco became a customer of Ace's inventory management system, and that resulted in savings to both companies.

Value propositions that include non-cash currencies take on many forms. Eric Bobby, founder and CEO of CityKi <www.cityki.com>, a network of kiosks designed to offer inner-city residents access to computer technology, goods, services, and information not readily available in their communities, has become very skilled in using currencies other than cash to build his business. This has allowed him to engage with companies who otherwise would not have done business with his early-stage venture. Here is how Eric describes an important relationship he's developed:

> We've built a relationship with a company that performs much of the software programming for the cable industry. And they are trying to use their software to move into managing media content on overhead advertising screens—like you see in airports. They are willing to work with us without cash compensation to develop and manage media content for the advertising screens on CityKi kiosks in order to further their own proficiencies in this new and emerging market. As a customer, we get their technology and they get a customer to help them develop a new product.

Eric goes on to describe how he secured the first physical location for a CityKi kiosk:

> We are currently in a grocery store that serves about 1,500 people a day. Part of the value proposition we intend to offer to local merchants is that a CityKi kiosk will increase foot traffic in their stores. However, that isn't the case yet. With this [grocery] store, the owner is very progressive. He opened this store seven years ago at a time when this was a desolate area. The store, as a cornerstone of the community, has really brought the whole area to life.
>
> So what is his interest in having us there? Before our machine was there, there was a gumball machine and hair care products. Now you see a state-of-the-art, beautiful, high-tech machine. And it looks a little out of

place. But at the same time, residents of the community realize what it is and they are very proud of it. And the owner of the store is very proud of it as well. He's proud of the community and wants to serve it better. He believes, as do we, that the kiosk is a vehicle through which we can bring needed services into the community. Long term, he feels he will generate commissions from the kiosk. But right now, he's giving us space for free and advertising for us because he thinks it is good for the community, and that is important to him.

Certainly, the type of value exchange explained above doesn't take place in a single, anonymous transaction. It takes the work of building trust with the other party through delivering the value promised time and again. It is all about building relationships.

CHOREOGRAPHERS MONETIZE *EVERY* RELATIONSHIP

When you have the mindset of an entrepreneur, you look for ways to either save money or make money in every interaction. With the skills of a choreographer, you look to bring together parties to the transaction that will actually do the work, satisfy the customers, and allow you to still profit from the transaction! The best way to help explain how our concept of Collaborative Communities is being operationalized is through an example of a Boston-based choreographer, Circles. Circles is the "leading provider of loyalty management programs." It offers relationship and loyalty marketing services to companies that make these services available to their customers and/or employees.

For example, suppose your largest customer is coming to town, and you want to have a special gift basket in her hotel room when she arrives. Circles will do the job. How? Because

Circles has created a Collaborative Community of business partners to provide a wide variety of products and services to its customers. Thus, once your request is received, Circles goes to its
already-vetted supplier of gift baskets and arranges for the basket to be made up and delivered.

But here's the interesting part. Because Circles views its gift
basket supplier as a customer as well as a business partner, it receives a payment from the supplier/customer for producing and
delivering the order to your customer's hotel room. Rather than
just buying a gift basket from a gift basket supplier, Circles has
in effect transformed that supplier into a customer. Circles
thereby derives monetary value from the gift basket supplier in
two ways: (1) by lowering its cost of fulfillment by having the
supplier provide the gift basket, and (2) by receiving a payment
from the supplier in return for giving it an order.

You might ask, Doesn't the supplier object to sharing its revenue from the order with Circles? Not at all. As Janet Kraus, the
cofounder and CEO of Circles says, "Our partners pay for the
business *and* they carry the cost of fulfilling the order. But they
don't object to the charge because," as Janet continues, "where our
partner previously had a customer acquisition cost of $100, it is
now $5." Sounds to us as though everyone comes out ahead.

As a choreographer, you should derive revenue from everyone in your community. The choreographer earns revenue in the
form of either cost savings or income generation from every customer and from every member firm/business partner (now
viewed as a customer). Deriving revenue from member firms is
a matter of identifying the value proposition that you, the choreographer, bring to any given member and the currencies,
whether cash or non-cash, that underlie the value proposition.

In building value propositions between yourself, as the
choreographer, and the business partners/members in your
community, it is important to remember that what these partners
offer are their competencies. They are specialists. The partner
often assumes responsibility for the cost of the competency it

brings into the community, thereby lowering the cost of that competency for the rest of the community. For example, because Circles assumes the cost of acquiring corporate customers and brings consumers to the suppliers, we've seen that it lowers the suppliers' customer acquisition costs. And because the suppliers have the expertise in fulfillment and assume that cost, Circles' cost of fulfillment is thereby lowered as well. Consequently, as member firms (including the choreographer) are able to piggy-back on the costs of other member firms that they would normally incur if operating on their own, each member firm reduces its total costs and therefore operates more profitably than would otherwise be possible.

If the choreographer can go to a member firm that handles the shipping and say, "I will give you information that will allow you to better manage your purchasing and inventory costs and, in return for receiving that information, I ask that you grant me a discount," the shipper will opt into the community as long as the savings from the opportunity outweigh the cost of the discount. So it's important to understand how best to use your access to information to help determine the proper ratio between the fee and the revenue opportunity, always remembering that member firms must make a profit or they will opt out of the community, thus weakening the entire community.

For member firms, choreographers offer many advantages, particularly in terms of sharing the cost of operations that touch the end customer. This savings can take the form of providing publicity and advertising services, analyses of customer purchasing data, software, professional or technical services such as assistance in process design and development, or even obtaining basic connectivity. As the community grows, the choreographer's value proposition to member firms grows through its increased knowledge and experience that allows it to better communicate the needs and wants of the end customer and the timing of those needs and wants. In this way, member firms can more easily determine their business model, infrastructure, and resource needs, and the goal of the community—satisfying customers' changing personal needs and wants profitably—can be achieved.

As with so much of life, it's really a matter of perspective. By viewing yourself as a choreographer and everyone you interact with as a customer, it is possible to derive revenue where before you saw only costs and at the same time enhance the value of your business and customer relationships. As we are fond of saying . . . business is a dance with the customer and the customer always leads.

WHAT HAVE WE LEARNED?

1 ▌ Our premise is that to achieve and maintain success in today's customer-centric era of collaborative business, *every* relationship must take on the characteristics of a customer relationship.

2 ▌ Customers have the power because increasingly they can choose with whom they do business and under what terms.

3 ▌ Increasingly, you have to look at your business from the perspective of your individual customers and present them with the solution that exactly fits their needs. If you don't provide it, your competitors will.

4 ▌ Just as you should build your business to satisfy the needs and wants of your primary customers, we also believe that you should look at all your business relationships with a customer focus and examine your business from their perspective.

5 ▌ By viewing everyone as a customer, you are in essence looking to develop longer-term, collaborative relationships as opposed to arms-length, transaction-based relationships. More important, you're

developing learning relationships that build trust by continually following through on promises made.

6 ▮ By viewing everyone as a customer, you fundamentally change the nature of the value proposition that exists between you and the entities with whom you interact. The value accruing from the bidirectional flow of goods, services, information, access, and money should increase for all concerned.

7 ▮ Only the recipient can assess the relative value in something he or she receives. And in many instances non-cash currencies can be of equal or greater utility than cash in achieving certain goals.

8 ▮ When you have the mindset of an entrepreneur, you look for ways to either save money or make money in every interaction. With the skills of a choreographer, you aim at bringing together parties to the transaction that will actually do the work, satisfy the customers, and allow you to still profit from the transaction.

9 ▮ As the community grows, the choreographer's value proposition to member firms grows through its increased knowledge and experience that allows it to better communicate the needs and wants of the end customer and the timing of those needs and wants.

10 ▮ By viewing yourself as a choreographer and everyone you interact with as a customer, it is possible to derive revenue where before you saw only costs and at the same time enhance the value of your business and customer relationships.

CHAPTER 4

It's All about Relationships

At its essence, whether automated or personal, in business or in war, collaboration exists only within the context of an ongoing relationship between and among people. Consequently, the foundation of collaborative business lies not in the tools that produce and transfer information and products but in the underlying human relationships that are ultimately responsible for the activities that take place within a collaboration.

As such, the measurements needed to manage collaborative relationships are different from those used for transactional relationships. Building effective collaborative relationships requires new skills and new measurement tools so they can be managed for both risk and advantage.

WHY COLLABORATE?

Think back to the business-centric era when it made sense for companies to organize around product lines. Under that type of company structure, it was inevitable, actually even desirable, to structure a company and its incentive compensation system on a product division–by–product division basis. Thus, companies not only fostered a win-lose attitude in their dealings with external businesses but their structures and incentive systems fostered that same mindset and culture within the company.

Despite the many benefits of collaborating across functional departments, product divisions, and externally with customers and business partners, most managers are inwardly focused. They seek efficiencies through reducing costs and cycle time, for example, trying to improve and automate purchasing. But growth and innovation don't come from reducing costs. Truly leveraging the benefits of collaboration requires reaching out across traditional boundaries and searching for win-win solutions to customer needs and business problems, a way of thinking that doesn't come naturally to people trained and motivated to act autonomously.

OBSTACLES TO EFFECTIVE COLLABORATION

Just as the majority of alliances and partnerships have failed, so too will most collaborative business efforts.

Why? Cultural impediments.

It is our view that existing organizational structures, incentive systems, and measurement frameworks, by and large, continue to foster win-lose attitudes at a time when win-win mindsets are needed. Collaboration means working together. Unfortunately, many people have trouble working together even in their own company, so how can they collaborate successfully with people in other companies? They can't. As a result, more and more companies are facing serious problems trying to profitably satisfy their customers.

A good indication of just how serious an impediment existing company culture and values can be is clear in a *Dilbert* comic strip (Figure 4.1).

FIGURE 4.1 | Cultural Impediments

Clearly, the loser in the I-win-you-lose game is the customer.

Most companies are challenged by the whole notion of collaboration. They have failed at their own internal collaboration initiatives because of (1) an organizational structure that creates silos; (2) the inability to get people to see the value of collaboration; and (3) the lack of a culture and a compensation system that foster working together to achieve shared goals. Collaboration requires a mindset that understands partnership and understands win-win value propositions.

An enlightening picture of how companies value important relationships is revealed in an Andersen–DYG study released in May 2001 <www.andersen.com/webs> of 500 C-level executives from United States–based publicly traded corporations across all industry sectors.

Customer Relationships

- Ninety-five percent of the executives said that "acquiring and maintaining relationships with customers" is essential to business success.

- Only 62 percent say they measure "customer turnover," only 43 percent measure "cost of customer acquisition," and only 44 percent think it is necessary to measure cost of customer acquisition in the future.

Employee Relationships

- Ninety-four percent of the executives said that "hiring and retaining the right employees" is essential to business success.

- Yet only 43 percent of them said their respective companies had a strategy in place to hire and retain the required head count and skill level.

Supplier Relationships

- Only 41 percent of the respondents said that "securing and maintaining relationships with suppliers" is essential to success, and only 49 percent said that "optimizing distribution channels" is essential.

- And whereas just 40 percent of companies currently have systems to "manage relationships with suppliers," only 23 percent have processes in place to measure the cost effects of "supplier turnover."

- And perhaps what is most surprising, only 17 percent of the respondents feel it is important to measure "supplier turnover" in the future.

As can be seen, although the vast majority of senior executives believe that relationships are essential to the long-term success of their business, these sources of value are largely overlooked and often inadequately managed. This neglect occurs despite the fact that, according to the Andersen–DYG study, "Nearly three-quarters of the market value of today's most successful companies is built upon sources of value that can be classified as relationship based or as intangibles, including people, ideas, knowledge, innovation, and relationships with customers, suppliers, and employees."

Nevertheless, adopting collaborative business practices is perceived by many companies as a risky proposition. For example, according to an *InformationWeek* research survey published May 7, 2001, most businesses don't routinely collaborate with customers and suppliers. Only one-half of the survey respondents said they regularly share information with customers, and only 37 percent routinely share information with suppliers.

As discussed in Chapter 1, we have entered the era of collaborative business, and collaborative business is practiced in trading communities. As such, companies that continue to resist collaborative initiatives will increasingly find themselves isolated and unable to satisfy their customers' personal needs and wants. So rather than continuing with the status quo of legacy thinking and thus sliding down the slippery slope to failure, all companies, both old and new, large and small, public or private, must embrace collaboration.

> ▌**Companies that resist collaborative initiatives** will find themselves isolated and unable to satisfy their customers.

THE PROBLEM: AN EXAMPLE AND THE SOLUTION

From our recent dealings with many companies across a range of industries, we know that the autonomous mindset and culture no longer work. Let's look at a typical example based on a composite of traditional companies. Company A is struggling with how to satisfy its customers' newly expressed desire for a single comprehensive solution rather than its traditional multiple-product approach. As currently structured, the company is organized around autonomous and somewhat competitive product line divisions. And while this structure and its underlying incentive systems have worked extremely well, today the company's customers, like customers in all industries in which the product is easily digitized, now expect the company to provide a solution tailored exactly to their needs rather than providing a variety of choices, some of which are better than others but none of which is exactly what they want. Unfortunately, the internal divisions of the company that turn out the multiple-product lines are not integrated sufficiently to provide the degree of collaboration necessary to create a single, highly personalized solution.

Consequently, realizing that change is needed and believing that collaboration is required, top management made collaborative business a strategic mandate. Yet shortly after the mandate was announced, the president of one division approached the president of another division to see if they could share customer lists. The request was denied. Needless to say, the president who made the request came away from the interaction flabbergasted. After all, to him the request was reasonable given top management's directive, and it seemed to him both divisions would benefit from working together.

Why didn't it happen?

Just because a company decrees that employees should henceforth collaborate doesn't mean that they can or will. What the company hasn't done is examine the existing impediments to collaboration. Specifically, the company has made no real changes to its autonomous product line divisional structure and underlying evaluation and compensation systems. Furthermore, despite its mandate, the company's win-lose competitive culture has remained intact.

Here's what we think should be done.

First and foremost, companies need to realize that collaboration doesn't mean just the integration of systems; it means the integration of people, and, unlike machines, people need incentives. This need for incentives is why everyone in the company must understand that collaboration requires a win-win relationship. And a win-win outcome in a collaborative relationship means both parties realize strategic benefit. Thus, *the real incentive for forming a collaborative relationship is a value proposition that brings increased strategic value to each party.* And strategic value is created whenever an exchange helps each party more quickly and less expensively validate or invalidate the critical assumptions they've made about how they intend to accomplish their goals.

> ∎ **The incentive for forming a** collaborative relationship is a value proposition that brings increased strategic value to each party.

Let's take a closer look at this important concept. A continuous stream of value propositions is required to get you and the other party closer and closer to your respective goals. However,

the only way to create that continuous stream of value propositions is by continually learning. And the way to learn (that is, the
way to get smart quickly for short dollars) is by validating or in-
validating the underlying assumptions about how you intend to
achieve your goals and the currencies those activities require. Or,
in other words, the value proposition you strike with the other
party is the flow of the currencies it makes available to you in return for the currencies you make available to it.

This means strategic value can be achieved through the exchange of currencies other than cash. Because this concept is so
important, let's discuss in more detail some of the points we
made only briefly in Chapter 3. *Webster's Dictionary* defines currencies as "(1) in circulation as a medium of exchange, and (2) a
common article for bartering."

> ▮ **Strategic value is created whenever** an exchange helps
> each party more quickly and less expensively validate or invali-
> date the critical assumptions they've made about their goals.

As we see it, a relationship between any two parties is
based on an underlying value proposition. Most simply, *a value
proposition* can be thought of as the bidirectional flow of currencies (goods, services, information, access, and money) between
the parties in a relationship. For example, if you purchased this
book from Amazon.com, the value proposition is you gave
them your money and they sent you this book (overnight if
you desired) at a discounted price. In other words, you gave
Amazon.com something they valued—your money—and they
gave you something you valued—this book delivered to you the
next day at a discounted price. What's important is that each
party receives something each values. And the recipient determines the value.

The party that gives you something may not view what it
gives as valuable and therefore feels that it "won" and you
"lost." But that type of attitude typifies legacy thinking and is

not conducive to collaboration. Obviously, it is irrelevant if you give something you do not value if the other party wants it. You may be perfectly satisfied and believe that you won. The truth is you both did, because you both received something to help you achieve your goals. However, because collaboration is built on qualities such as trust and cooperation, it is beneficial to encourage win-win thinking, as the required levels of trust and cooperation will not grow if one or both parties seeks to take advantage of the other. That kind of win-lose attitude inevitably manifests itself and destroys the collaboration. However, both parties having a win-win attitude also manifests itself, and the collaboration grows to the benefit of both parties.

But returning to Company A, its challenge is to restructure its autonomous product line–based divisions around sets of customer needs. Obviously, streamlining overlapping and competing product divisions is not something that happens overnight nor without pain. Collaboration reduces redundancies so many jobs may be eliminated and turf battles fought. But until the overall company structure is built from the customer's perspective— the desired single solution—a culture that fosters internal collaboration will not be achieved.

Information systems and workflows must be organized around the manner in which customers interact with the company. Decision making should be decentralized so that employees can act on the information presented by the company's information technology (IT) system. Training and education programs should emphasize the benefits of collaboration for the company and the individual employees. The company's compensation system should be revised to support collaborative efforts versus individual divisional performance rankings. This is a critical, yet often overlooked, element in any change effort. People naturally better perform the activities for which they are being compensated. For example, suppose a company rewards its sales staff based on total revenue generated; no incentive exists in that system for the staff to collaborate with others in the company and with suppliers to ensure that the product is produced and delivered to the customer in a timely manner and at the greatest profit to the company. Nor is there an incentive to work with colleagues in other divisions to plan a joint effort to understand customer needs and meet them efficiently.

Finally, the company must realize that building a relationship based on trust is an iterative process. You have to move from relationships where there is just enough faith to forge the contract at hand to relationships of confidence and finally to relationships based on proven trust. It doesn't happen overnight or because employees are told to collaborate or are given new collaborative tools.

CURRENCIES OTHER THAN CASH

As we just described, implicit in putting in place a win-win value proposition is the recognition and understanding that value can be realized through the exchange of currencies other than cash. We include as non-cash currencies such things as:

- Customers—People or business entities that buy your primary product or service.

- Products and services—Another party's primary product or service you make use of in achieving your goals.

- Competencies—People-embodied skills that are necessary for your community to function effectively.

- Validation—A testimonial to the value you offer or in support of your expertise.

- Technology—A manner of accomplishing a task, in particular, technical processes, methods, or knowledge.

- Intellectual property—Proprietary know-how.

These are the currencies we feel are most relevant within the context of a customer-centric, collaborative business. However, we realize that our list may not include some categories of non-cash currency you value and use, and that's OK. In fact, once you gain experience in more systematically tracking and using non-cash currencies, you'll most likely compose your own list. What is important, however, is for you to start to capture the ones you are using. Having done that, you can either replace one or more of the categories we identified or you can take our general category descriptions and make them more specific to better suit your needs.

Another interesting dimension of currencies is that they can exist on three levels: information about, access to, or actual currency.

"Information about" means that you give or receive information regarding one of the currencies, for example, information about customers or information about a product or service.

"Access to" means that you give or receive access to one of the currencies, for example, access to customers or access to a product or service or access to technology.

"Actual currency" means that you are directly providing or receiving actual customers, the actual product or service, or the actual technology.

When you array these currencies against the three possible levels, you have what we call the Currency Grid shown in Figure 4.2. Let's look at this grid in more detail. (The following is but a short list of potential ways of obtaining currencies. In reality, how you obtain and use currencies is limited only by your creativity.)

Customers. Customers are probably the most freely traded non-cash currency. Your distribution partners provide you with actual customers for your primary products and services. Networking events, speaking engagements, referrals from colleagues, and publicity all provide you with access to potential customers, while information about customers can come from

FIGURE 4.2 | The Currency Grid

Currencies \ Levels	Information About	Access To	Actual Currency
Cash			
Customers			
Products and Services			
Competencies			
Validation			
Technology			
Intellectual Property			

many sources, including the media, colleagues, business partners, and so on. The people who provide you with these opportunities are important relationships because without customers you don't have a business.

Products and services. As we saw in Chapter 3, gain can be realized through cost savings as well as revenue generation. What you try to make use of with this currency are actual products and services that can be bartered directly or made available in exchange for evaluating and testing information about the product or service you provide to the seller that is beneficial to him. Software vendors often make use of this currency, providing early versions of products to users in exchange for feedback that allows them to improve the product before offering it for general sale. While actual is the most common form of the currency, access to products and services can come through membership in an exclusive group or through knowledge gained from colleagues. Information about products and services can come from anyone at any time—assuming you know what you need and are a good listener.

Competencies. Competencies are people-embodied skills. For example, if you know you need a really useful Web site to expand your business, one of the currencies you might need is the competency (skill) of Web site design. You may know a very good Web site designer—thereby potentially giving you the actual currency if you were to engage him or her. A colleague might introduce you to Web site design firms—giving you access to the currency. Finally, someone you know may recently have completed a major Web site project and thereby have a lot of information about the Web site design firms in your area—thus giving you "information about." Again, your interpersonal skills come into play. Regardless of the currency level (because by now we trust you understand the difference), gaining the competencies you need to build your community is a function of the people you know, your ability to understand what they can offer you, and your ability to craft the value proposition that will bring their currencies to the table.

Validation. Everyone wants to have at least one marquee customer. If you are working with Dell or IBM, certainly you've passed the company's due diligence and thus are known to offer a good product and good value. Validation can also come from being quoted as an expert or from publishing your thoughts on a topic in a respected industry journal. The relationships that can provide you with that validation directly allow you access to the stage or publication through which you obtain that validation; or, finally, information about opportunities to obtain validation become critical relationships for establishing and maintaining your credibility.

Technology. We include technology as a currency because of the critical role it plays in supporting human collaboration. Technology allows people in separate locations to work together and to share processes and information across corporate boundaries. Collaborative technologies promise to open up new opportunities and reduce costs, yet they often require significant investment. Relationships that can bring you needed technologies are important to any community.

Intellectual property. Sir Francis Bacon was right: knowledge is power. Relationships that allow you the use of someone else's intellectual property, such as a patented process or method important to your work, or that build your own proprietary know-how can help you reduce licensing costs or perhaps simply gain you access that you wouldn't receive if you were a stranger.

So as you look at your relationships, examine the currencies they offer you and think about what you need to build your community. Remember that in any human endeavor you can identify non-cash currencies—perhaps other than those identified here—that help you get closer to your goal. Your job is to identify these relationship currencies and who has them, when you need them, and then strike the value proposition that allows you access to them.

USING NON-CASH RELATIONSHIP CURRENCIES

By now you may think that we value non-cash currencies more than cash. We don't. We value them equally. Of course, in order to function either as an individual or as a business requires cash. How much cash and when it's needed depends on your particular situation.

A truism about business, however, is that the barter system will never die. Many business relationships have been, and will continue to be, based on non-cash currencies, so you need to understand how to utilize them. Before we get into more detail, here's a simple example that we were recently presented with. We had sent out an e-mail announcement to a subset of our contact database about a workshop we were running. No sooner had it been sent then we received the following note:

> I just received the invitation for the December 4th event. I would like to attend but I do not have the money to pay for a ticket. Business has been extremely slow for me this year, and I've had to cut back on many things. Given this, I was wondering if there is anything I could do to barter or trade for the cost of the event. I have lots of skills, but without having any idea of what you might need, I'm not sure what to offer. Please let me know if this is a possibility, and if it is, let's set up a time to talk about what would be a fair trade.

Clearly, everyone makes use of relationship currencies in the value propositions they strike, but realizing their value is a skill that must be practiced and developed. And as we've stressed, it requires looking at any value proposition from a customer's perspective. Although our note sender certainly had collaboration in mind, let's look at it from a different perspective. Her message was about what *she* wanted and asked *us* to identify the value proposition. Fair enough. She was certainly headed in a collaborative direction. However, what she might have done better was to think about our needs in running a workshop, such as customers to fill the seats, and then what currencies she could have offered to help meet those needs. For example, she could offer to pass on our invitation to her contact list with a personal note.

Some Win-Win Examples

Successfully dealing in non-cash, relationship currencies requires you to think about things in terms of win-win activities. Which is exactly what Ruth Owades of Caylx & Corolla did in 1991 when she approached FedEx about partnering with her young company to deliver flowers direct from growers around the world to individual consumers. Because part of the value proposition she offered to her consumers was that her flowers were fresher and thus would last longer than those available from other vendors, she knew she needed to reduce the length of shipping time. With its global reach and efficient processes, FedEx was her preferred shipper. The only problem was that FedEx didn't ship perishables. So Ruth did her homework, learning about the quantities of perishables moving about the world and the amount of business they could potentially represent to FedEx. She then approached the company with the following value proposition: "Work with me to learn how to ship perishables and I'll not only give you my business, it'll help you develop a new service that will help you grow your business." Essentially what she offered was an actual customer (her company) and a new service in exchange for a service she needed. Today, 11 years later, Caylx & Corolla still ships its flowers via FedEx and the global shipment of perishables has expanded significantly.

Now let's take a closer look at how you utilize relationship currencies. First, you don't have to convert all non-cash currencies into cash because in many instances non-cash currencies have greater utility than cash. However, in order to use these non-cash currencies, you need to identify what you have that can be of value to the other party. You then have to identify another person/company that can use the non-cash currency. It is also essential to understand that you can use the non-cash currencies you have (whether they were yours to begin with or you received them from someone else) in value propositions you are setting up with other parties.

■ **Strategic value can be achieved** through the exchange of currencies other than cash.

For example, as we mentioned in the preface, we had the good fortune in June 2001 to be keynote speakers at the Collaborative Commerce Summit. We knew that in addition to any cash compensation we received, we would also receive third-party validation as experts in collaborative business and access to potential customers (the attendees at the summit). After the summit, we were able to derive non-cash value from the many relationships we established as a result of the publicity we received for being keynote speakers and attending the summit. (We'll look at this example in greater detail in Chapter 9.)

Let's now turn our attention to Verndale Corporation <www.verndalecorp.com>, a choreographer that helps its customers strategize, build, and manage Internet solutions to business problems. For most of their customers, Internet technology is not a core competency, so Joe Zarrett and Chris Pisapia, the company's founders, have designed their business to provide this competency in an integrated and seamless manner. They work hard at building the relationships that allow them to become their customers' "Web development department." Verndale's competitors include both free agents and major consulting firms, so Chris and Joe understand they can't win customers by offering the lowest price, nor can they afford the kind of marketing and advertising that would make their name as well known as that of many of their competitors. Instead, they made the decision to look for distribution partners that can help them reach their intended customers within their community. Their initial target: a business association with 900 members, many of whom, as Joe says, "live and breathe within the association. We understood the benefit of getting inside the organization, of becoming a vital partner to that organization. So we asked the executive director why the group didn't have a Web site and would she be interested in having us develop one for them. We knew, like most not-for-profit organizations, it didn't have a lot of cash, so we offered to develop a Web site for the association in exchange for the exposure it would give us."

Verndale quickly developed a Web site for this organization and continues to maintain it, thus exchanging actual product and competencies for access to customers—that is, the members of the organization. In addition, the organization offers actual validation as it is a well-known and highly respected group. The trick is to convert the non-cash currencies Verndale receives into value that helps Verndale achieve its goals. In tracking the currencies and relationships that have led to cash and helped the company realize its goals, Joe offers the following comments:

> It took about six to eight months before we realized cash directly from this relationship. In addition, we've generated a great deal of exposure and subsequently a good many of our customers have come through this channel. We've received validation and access to customers when we've spoken at events where the topic has been e-commerce. In fact, one of our largest customers came directly from one of these events. We also met a gentleman who has become a great spokesperson for us. He has brought us many very qualified leads that have resulted in at least eight customers. In return, we've supported him and some of his customers without charge.
>
> Our relationship has continued for about two years. It has been a true partnership. We continue to do work on a heavily discounted rate—often for no cash compensation. They continue to provide us with access to customers in exchange for our services. We're now listed as a sustaining partner. Our logo is attached to every piece of collateral they send to their members.

Verndale's relationship with this organization began with non-cash currencies that they converted into needed value with other parties. But relationships don't always have to take this path. Joe offers us another example of using non-cash currencies to gain access to customers, this time beginning with a customer that pays in cash:

> We went into our kickoff meeting and as we walked by the sales department, I saw list after list of the top com-

panies in the area, color-coded to represent both their current customers and the customers they wanted. I recognized what a gold mine that was and that my job was to gain access to their customers. We went through a very successful project with our customer, and at the end of the project we approached the director of marketing about doing a joint direct mail piece to announce the launch of the site. We offered to design it without charge and to share the printing costs if they would distribute it and include a description of our services. They agreed. We introduced them to another of our customers, a printing company, that gave us a great rate on the piece. It has just been sent to 5,500 potential customers at a cash cost to us of 16 cents a piece!

What's more, the printing company and our other customer will now be working together. They do a number of education programs and so they have a large amount of collateral printed. So we were able to make the connection between two of our customers and get our names in front of thousands of people.

Nice collaboration, Joe!

THE TRUST IMPERATIVE

Even though collaborative relationships must be centered on understanding and meeting the needs of the parties involved, successful relationships begin with a clear sense of exactly what you can do for your business partner and what your partner can do for you. The more you know about your partner's needs, preferences, and aspirations, the better you can create mutually beneficial trusting relationships.

We'll discuss this in more detail in Chapter 8, but you collaborate with people you trust because you can share knowledge and deal with issues more quickly from having such a close relationship. Trusting that your business partners will behave responsibly with shared information—and agreeing on what constitutes responsible behavior—is absolutely critical to the success of collaborative business. Ethical behavior in collaboration boils down to business partners setting expectations up front about the relationship and the sharing of information and then meeting the expectations. It's simply doing what you say you're going to do and knowing that your partners will do the same.

VALUING RELATIONSHIPS

The skills required for forming collaborative relationships are identifying the relationships that provide you the greatest benefit and then bringing to those relationships a continuous stream of value propositions that produce increasing value for each party. The challenges these requirements create for you are fivefold:

1. How to evaluate relationships and the currencies they can provide from the perspective of their ability to help you achieve your goals

2. How to understand what the other person needs and how you can provide it

3. How to structure a value proposition that allows you to access the currencies

4. Identifying the required level of resources to allocate to a relationship in order to fulfill current value propositions

5. Identifying the next one in the continuous stream of value propositions that allows each party to move closer toward its goals

As we said in Chapter 2, regardless of whether you are an individual free agent, an entrepreneur, a corporate manager, or an executive, the challenges today are exactly the same. Oh sure, we appreciate the fact there are many differences between being a free agent or part of a large organization, but when you boil it down, the skill required for success—the ability to identify the most important relationships and then bring to those relationships a continuous stream of value propositions that produce increasing value for each party in the relationship—is exactly the same. We also understand that many businesspeople appreciate the importance of relationships and the use of non-cash currencies, but as collaboration becomes increasingly essential to success, haphazard evaluation no longer suffices. To truly benefit you have to become rigorous with all relationship currencies, valuing and measuring them in a precise and systematic way.

THE CHALLENGE

It is interesting that most business thinkers see the need for collaboration but emphasize that the key to successful collaboration is technology. Certainly, the technical advances that first permitted different departments within a company to share information and then to connect with constituents external to the company are a major factor in the push for collaboration. For example, analysts tout the benefits of "collaborative commerce," describing it as the marriage of enterprise resource planning (ERP), customer relationship management (CRM), supply chain management (SCM), and e-procurement technologies. The integration challenges discussed at business conferences on collaboration often center on linking data warehouses or newly developed CRM systems to legacy financial applications. We recognize the need for technological innovation and integration (and we will talk about it in Chapter 8), but the key to collaboration is not the integration of data systems. It is the integration of human beings. It's about relationships.

■ **The key to collaboration is not** the integration of data systems. It is the integration of human beings. It's about relationships.

Yet relationships are intangible and thus difficult to value and measure. The value in relationships is rarely accounted for or disclosed in a company's financial statements. In fact, despite the existence of accounting standards for recording or disclosing information about intangible assets, traditional accounting measures will never reflect the true value in relationships because they simply can't be measured in dollars and cents.

So how do you do it? How do you look at the myriad human relationships that you have and determine whether they are adding value?

Because of the question's importance, we have looked at this issue carefully and have developed a method we feel is accurate and relatively easy. In the next chapter, we begin to discuss it.

WHAT HAVE WE LEARNED?

1 ■ Most companies are challenged by the whole notion of collaboration. They have failed at their own internal collaboration initiatives because of (1) an organizational structure that creates silos; (2) the inability to get people to see the value of collaboration; and (3) the lack of a culture and an incentive compensation system that foster working together to achieve shared goals.

2 ■ Companies that continue to resist collaborative initiatives will increasingly find themselves isolated and unable to satisfy their customers' personal needs and wants.

3 ■ Companies must realize that collaboration doesn't mean just the integration of systems; it means the integration of people, and, unlike machines, people need incentives. This need for incentives is why everyone in the company must understand that collaboration requires a win-win relationship.

4 ∎ The real incentive for forming a collaborative relationship is a value proposition that brings increased strategic value to each party. And strategic value is created whenever an exchange helps each party more quickly and less expensively validate or invalidate the critical assumptions they've made about how they intend to accomplish their goals.

5 ∎ Strategic value can be achieved through the exchange of currencies other than cash.

6 ∎ A value proposition can be thought of as the bidirectional flow of currencies (goods, services, information, access, and money) between the people in a relationship.

7 ∎ An interesting dimension of currencies is that they can exist on three levels: information about, access to, or actual currency.

8 ∎ You don't have to convert all non-cash currencies into cash because in many instances non-cash currencies have greater utility than cash. However, in order to use these non-cash currencies, you have to identify what you have that can be of value to the other party.

9 ∎ Trusting that your business partners will behave responsibly with shared information—and agreeing on what constitutes responsible behavior—is absolutely critical to the success of collaborative business. Ethical behavior in collaboration boils down to business partners setting expectations up front about the relationship and the sharing of information and then meeting the expectations.

10 ∎ The skills required for forming collaborative relationships are identifying the relationships that provide you the greatest benefit and then bringing to those relationships a continuous stream of value propositions that produce increasing value for each party.

11 ∎ The key to collaboration is not the integration of data systems. It is the integration of human beings. It's about relationships.

PART TWO

Purposeful
Collaboration

CHAPTER 5

Not All Relationships Are the Same

We ended the last section with a brief description of the challenge facing everyone in business, whether a free agent or a corporate executive: to identify his or her most important relationships and then bring to those relationships a continuous stream of value propositions that produce increasing value for each person in the relationship.

However, as we've discussed, businesses have found that collaborative relationships are not easily quantified and controlled.

THE SOLUTION

Observing the problem, we developed an iterative method for effectively analyzing the underlying relationships in business, thereby allowing you to correctly evaluate which relationships offer the greatest value. We refer to this method as *Purposeful Collaboration*—a process that allows you to trade in relationship currencies that clearly help both parties move toward their respective goals. Consequently, the objective of purposeful collaboration is to create a win-win relationship while engaging in activities that satisfy both parties' customers and build a profitable business.

When you enter into purposeful collaboration, you clearly identify the purpose of the interaction. It allows you to understand what you have that is of value to the other party and specifically what you seek from the business relationship with the other party. With this knowledge, you can allocate the proper resources (time, energy, and currencies) to your most important relationships and thereby improve your performance and achieve your goals. However, in order to manage your relationships in this fashion, you first need to measure what you are receiving from each of your relationships. And to do that, you have to establish values.

■ **Purposeful collaboration allows you to** understand what you have that is of value to the other party and specifically what you seek from him or her.

How do you value what you receive from a relationship?

You start by analyzing *every* business relationship with respect to (1) the *nature* of the relationship and (2) the *rhythm* of the relationship. We use these two perspectives because the nature of the relationship indicates how important a relationship is for achieving your goals, whereas the rhythm of the relationship provides a sense of your commitment of resources to that relationship.

By evaluating every relationship from these two perspectives, you can sort each relationship into one of the four quadrants shown in Figure 5.1.

When using the Relationship Matrix, first keep in mind that it is designed from *your* perspective, not the other party's. However, having said that, we need to stress that because everyone you interact with should be viewed as a customer, the "other

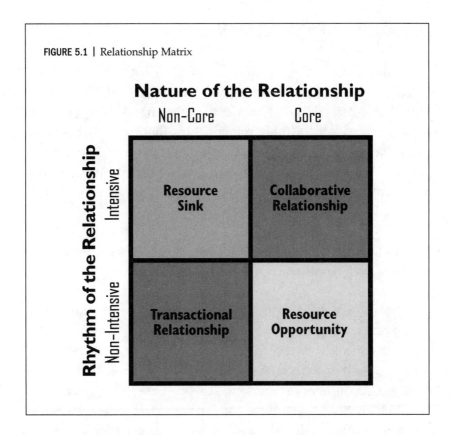

FIGURE 5.1 | Relationship Matrix

Nature of the Relationship

Non-Core   Core

Rhythm of the Relationship

Intensive

Resource Sink | Collaborative Relationship

Non-Intensive

Transactional Relationship | Resource Opportunity

party" should be thought of with that mindset, encouraging you to think of their needs, as you would any customer. Second, when you categorize your relationships into one of the four quadrants, you do so at a particular moment. In essence, just as a balance sheet reflects the financial condition of a business at a specific time (for example, as of December 31, 2002), so too does the Relationship Matrix. Thus, if you examine your relationships on December 31, 2002, and then again on January 31, 2003, some of those relationships may have shifted into a new quadrant as a result of the interactions that occurred during the month of January.

Now let's take a closer look at the matrix (Figure 5.1) and see how we define its two axes.

THE NATURE OF THE RELATIONSHIP

The nature of the relationship refers to whether you are receiving currencies that help you achieve your goals. If you are, then that relationship is core. On the other hand, non-core relationships are all those other relationships that play a supporting role in your business and don't relate directly to achieving your goals. That doesn't mean they are not important on their own terms; rather, it simply means they are not currently core to your business.

> ▮ **The nature of the relationship** refers to whether you are receiving currencies that help you achieve your goals.

Setting S-M-A-R-T goals. When identifying your goals, make sure every goal passes the "S-M-A-R-T" test. Make sure your goals are **S**pecific, **M**easurable, **A**ttainable, **R**elevant, and **T**ime sensitive. And even though our process helps you achieve whatever goals you deem important, it's our belief that your goals should be related to the three core business processes that make up the business model of a customer-centric, collaborative business: (1) customer acquisition and retention—how you get and keep your customers; (2) product and service innovation—how you continually generate the solutions your customers desire; and (3) customer fulfillment and service—how you deliver to and service your customers. Therefore, to trade in relationship currencies and use your resources most effectively, you *must* focus on those relationships that help you carry out your core processes.

> ▮ **Make sure your goals are:** Specific, Measurable, Attainable, Relevant, and Time sensitive.

For example, you may use specific goals, such as signing up 100 new customers in the next six months or finding a contract manufacturer to produce a new product or finding a distribution partner, and so forth. In fact, this goal-setting task is a powerful tool for creating alignment throughout an organization. The CEO may set broad goals, which then can be used as guidelines for establishing the more narrowly defined goals of the individuals responsible for carrying out the activities that in the aggregate achieve the company's broader goals.

CUSTOMERS CAN BE NON-CORE RELATIONSHIPS

Right now you may be thinking that all your customers must be core relationships as one of the core processes is customer acquisition and retention. But that isn't quite correct. Customer relationships can be non-core if the only exchange of value is their paying you for your product and service and your fulfilling and servicing their needs in the normal daily course of your business. Although your business depends on customers like these for continued financial health, they may not be core to achieving your company's current goals relative to expansion or addressing new business challenges. Again we come back to the question of alignment of goals throughout the organization. If you're the CEO, such customers may not be core relationships on which to focus your personal energies as you go about achieving the broader goals of the company. However, keeping customers that routinely purchase without a fuss may be the most important goal of the vice president of customer relationships.

UNDERSTANDING THE *RHYTHM* OF RELATIONSHIPS

The *rhythm* of a relationship relates to the patterned flow and intensity of the interactions between you and the other party. According to *Webster's Dictionary*, *intensive* means "constituting or relating to a method designed to increase productivity by the expenditure of more capital and labor." Therefore, if the interactions you have with the other person—whether face-to-face or by e-mail or telephone—take place on a regular and intense basis, we characterize them as intensive. If the interactions are intermittent and limited, we characterize them as non-intensive. Because every interaction involves the use of your limited resources—time, energy, and currencies—the rhythm of a relationship is a reflection of the resources committed to that relationship. Intensive relationships tend to use lots of resources; non-intensive relationships use fewer resources.

> ■ **The *rhythm* of a relationship** relates to the patterned flow and intensity of the interactions in a relationship and reflects the resources committed to that relationship.

As we've discussed, collaboration requires strong and trusting relationships, which generally require an intensive rhythm. Accordingly, look at all your relationships and assess whether the commitment of resources to each is appropriate given its value. For example, for a non-core relationship, seek to minimize the commitment of resources through centralizing contact, streamlining processes, introducing technology, and so on. For a core relationship, commit the resources needed to ensure that both parties build the trust required to achieve strategic and financial benefit.

Purposeful collaboration, whether with customers or business partners, requires strong and trusting relationships. And, as we've said, while these types of relationships consume resources for their development and nurturing, they are worthwhile. With each interaction, each party's intent is to get closer to achieving individual and mutual goals. Any other mindset doesn't lead to the desired results for either party.

Even though these relationships are intensive, in the long run, if done correctly, they allow you to conserve your resources. As each party in the collaboration is contributing its core competencies, each party is thus saving by focusing on those aspects of its business that are most important and that it can accomplish most effectively. No, you're not going to find that elusive 25th hour in the day. But whenever you save, you are implicitly creating because saving time, money, and energy increases your freedom to get more things done.

The real incentive for forming collaborative relationships, therefore, is a value proposition that brings increased value to each party, and value is created when an exchange of currencies helps you improve the efficiency and effectiveness of your core business processes. That is, you can more quickly and less expensively validate or invalidate the assumptions on which you designed your core processes. Or, put another way, a relationship has value, even if cash doesn't change hands, if it helps you more quickly and less expensively validate or invalidate the critical assumptions you've made about your primary customers and your business model—what your business does and how it intends to make money.

Recall the relationships Eric Bobby of CityKi has struck with the technology vendor and the grocery store owner. One of Eric's assumptions about how he'll generate revenue from the merchants and service providers represented on his kiosks is by providing them with prominent advertising opportunities. By working with his technology vendor to develop and manage the media content of CityKi's overhead screens, Eric can quickly validate or invalidate that assumption. Another of Eric's assumptions about how to bring users to his kiosks is to locate them in high-traffic, safe locations like a grocery store, which people frequent on a regular basis. He also believes it is important that his initial kiosks are hosted by merchants who are respected in the community. So the grocery store owner where he placed the first kiosk is helping him to validate these important assumptions regarding customer acquisition. Accordingly, both relationships have great value to Eric, even though no cash has changed hands.

Now let's see how we characterize each of the four relationship types shown in Figure 5.1.

TRANSACTIONAL RELATIONSHIPS

A transactional relationship is a non-core relationship that has a non-intensive rhythm. The frequency of interaction between you and the other party is relatively low and requires a minimum level of resources. Look at it as if you and the other person are essentially in balance. You're not receiving something of core value but then neither are you using a lot of resources, and the same is true of the other person. Sometimes transactional relationships are referred to as "arm's-length relationships" in that the parties do not have a relationship beyond the minimum required to carry out the specific transaction. Clearly, all of us have many necessary transactional relationships, even if they are not core.

It is also important to appreciate that a relationship remaining in the transactional quadrant over the long run is perfectly acceptable and in fact expected. For example, you probably consider your relationship with the landlord of space you rent as transactional. On the first of every month you send the landlord a check, and the landlord makes sure you have occupancy of the rented space as specified in the lease. Having a transactional relationship does not imply anything about your relationship other than you are not committing a lot of resources, because the currencies used in the value proposition do not add core value.

RESOURCE SINK RELATIONSHIPS

A relationship characterized as a resource sink is one in which the value accruing to you from the relationship is not core, as is the case in a transactional relationship. However, unlike a transactional relationship, there is an intensive rhythm in a resource sink relationship. As we said, relationships that have an intensive rhythm generally consume a lot of resources. And relationships that use a lot of resources but don't provide core benefits dissipate your time, energy, and currencies. A resource sink relationship is out of balance in that you give to, but do not get from, the relationship. More accurately, what you do receive is out of proportion to what you expend. We can also look at this as a lose-win relationship because you're losing and you presume the other party is winning.

An example of a resource sink relationship. One of our customers is an agricultural business. The company's management is passionately committed to preserving farmland and stewardship of the land in general. As such, over the past few years the business has held a festival, the net proceeds of which it's donated to a not-for-profit organization, whose mission is to preserve open space and farmland. While it was (and is) very happy to make that contribution, it hadn't looked to see what the organization might offer in return that would benefit them both. Thus, our customer was giving more than it was getting, and even though personally satisfying, the relationship was a resource sink from a business standpoint.

We don't mean to imply anything negative about any person with whom you have this kind of relationship other than that it is wasting some of your resources. In fact, you may believe the relationship should be core, and thus you may be willing to invest resources to iterate it to a core relationship. Before we explained the situation, our customer knew intuitively its relationship with the not-for-profit was important but hadn't realized how to make it core to its business. In Chapter 8, we'll talk more about how the company is turning this valuable, but nonetheless resource sink, relationship into a collaborative one. For now, let's explain that if you allow an imbalance where you are giving more than you are getting to persist, you risk running out of resources. Consequently, you don't want to maintain a relationship in the resource sink quadrant. You must take action to change the situation because a resource sink is not a viable long-term type of relationship.

RESOURCE OPPORTUNITY RELATIONSHIPS

A relationship characterized as a resource opportunity provides core value even though the rhythm of your interaction with the other party is non-intensive, and you do not use a lot of your resources—the exact opposite of a resource sink relationship. You may view this as positive, and it is, but only if the other party continues to provide his or her currencies. However, unless the rhythm of your interaction becomes more intensive, you may not maintain the relationship. Essentially, what this relationship means is that the other party is providing currencies that help you achieve your goals, but currently you are not committing a sufficient level of resources to help the other party achieve his or her goals. Thus, you are getting more than you are giving. In that case, it's win-lose—you're winning and you presume the other party is losing. As such, this is not a viable state for a relationship over the long run.

An example of a resource opportunity relationship. Our colleague, Dave Blakelock, relates how he successfully recruited the athletic director of a major university to serve on the board of advisors of a sports-related business Dave had begun. Over time, the athletic director introduced Dave to several people who were important to Dave. Yet Dave didn't understand what benefit the athletic director was getting from their relationship. Dave didn't know what currency he was offering that was valuable to the athletic director, so he was hesitant to try to make the relationship more intensive. From Dave's perspective, he was winning and his associate was losing. Knowing that was not a viable state for the relationship, Dave asked why his associate continued to offer currencies when Dave was offering nothing in return. Surprised, the athletic director responded that Dave offered him the chance to participate in a business, something university life didn't offer. Now recognizing that both were receiving value, Dave was willing to commit greater resources to the relationship so that they both could receive even greater value from it.

COLLABORATIVE RELATIONSHIPS

A collaborative relationship is one in which the other party provides core value to you and you provide core value to him or her. And reflective of the value accruing to both, the rhythm of the relationship is intensive.

But remember that building a collaborative relationship is an iterative process. You have to move the relationship from one in which there is just enough faith to forge the contract at hand to a relationship of confidence and finally to a relationship of proven trust. Only then do you both have access to all the currencies the other can put on the table, so you both can benefit. (We'll discuss this point in more detail in Chapter 9.) Our agricultural business and the not-for-profit organization have begun down this path. Among other things, they are working on ways to jointly bring more customers to the farm and more members to the organization.

And similar to a transactional relationship, a relationship in the collaborative quadrant is viable because it is a win-win for both parties.

Thus, we can now see how all business relationships fall into one of the four quadrants. The resource sink and resource opportunity relationships are not long term in nature because of their lose-win and win-lose structure. (Remember, the quadrant is assigned from your perspective.) By contrast, transactional and collaborative relationships are viable win-win states. Having said that, you must keep in mind that over time your goals will change, and what is of value today may change tomorrow.

In addition, whom you want to build a collaborative relationship with is likely to change. Most important, never forget that achieving and maintaining success in business is a never-ending, iterative process.

Obviously, it is impossible for all your relationships to be collaborative. No one has a sufficient level of resources to maintain an intensive rhythm in every relationship. In fact, given the value that collaborative relationships bring and the resources involved in realizing that value, you'll probably maintain relatively few. You don't need every relationship to be collaborative to be successful. The ability to identify the most important relationships and then bring to those relationships a continuous stream of value propositions that produce increasing value for each party is what is important. And integral to enhancing those value propositions is the understanding and systematic use of cash and non-cash relationship currencies as well as a method of valuing, measuring, and managing the utility of those currencies.

▌ **Integral to enhancing value propositions** is the systematic use of relationship currencies as well as a method of valuing, measuring, and managing their utility.

CREATING A COLLABORATIVE RELATIONSHIP

Now that we understand the four different types of business relationships, let's take a look at how to turn a non-collaborative relationship into a collaborative one.

The first step is to map the value proposition of the existing relationship. By this we mean you spell out the *specific* value proposition that currently exists between you and the other party by identifying the bidirectional flow of goods, services, information, money, and access.

As an example, let's again take the relationship you have with your landlord. As we said, most likely you send the landlord a check on the first of every month, and in return the land-lord provides space and maintains it according to your lease. For many companies, rent is often one of their largest expenses, so their relationship with the landlord is important but not neces-sarily core.

Another example is derived from our interactions with a property owner and one of his business tenants. The tenant, Dave, saw an opportunity for his landlord relationship to have an impact on one of his core business processes. Dave believes that the other tenants of his landlord (Max) are potential cus-tomers for his (Dave's) shipping and logistics services. Dave un-derstands that if he can reach the landlord's 300 other tenants, he can reduce both the time and the cost to reach those potential customers. In other words, Dave can validate or invalidate his assumption that Max's tenants are his potential customers more quickly and for less money. But what's in it for Max? His busi-ness is developing and managing property, not offering some-one else's products to his tenants . . . or is it?

Dave understands that the power in business relationships has shifted to customers, and even in a tight real estate market, it is more economical for a tenant to renew a lease or move to an-other space under the same landlord than for the landlord to find a completely new tenant. So if Dave can help Max provide a value-added service to his tenants, wouldn't he be helping Max develop his relationship with his tenants? And couldn't that developing relationship result in greater customer retention *and* be turned into a new product offering and revenue stream for Max? After all, Dave was willing to pay for access to the ten-ants. Come to think of it, Dave's friend Myer is in the messenger business. Dave thought Myer might also want to offer services to Max's tenants.

Dave approached Max and discovered that Max had already been thinking how he could be of greater value to his tenants. He does want them to renew their leases rather than move on. And Max wants to differentiate himself in the marketplace and in the minds of real estate brokers. After his conversation with Dave, Max now understands that with 300 tenants in a dozen buildings located in the same city, he offers a distribution channel to vendors and can use that access to customers to get discounts and special services for his tenants/customers. So Max agreed to start to transform his and Dave's relationship. As the first iteration, Max included a flyer in his tenants' monthly bills announcing that Dave and his friend Myer would offer shipping, logistics, and messenger services at a reduced rate to tenants in Max's buildings. And Dave and Myer have agreed that after a trial period to assess tenants' interest, they will pay Max a fee for each tenant that becomes their customer. It's a small step but an important one. All three men have adopted a new perspective on their relationship; but keeping our focus on Dave and Max, we find they are expanding the exchange of value between them and turning a transactional non-core relationship into a collaborative one. And the benefit for both is that it immediately reduces the cost of customer acquisition for Dave (plus increases the value he gets from his rent) and provides Max with the beginning of a new service/product offering for his tenants (discounts and special services—starting with shipping, logistics, and messenger services as seen in Figure 5.2) that he believes will help him retain his tenants and provide a new revenue stream.

Now let's think about Dave and Max's relationship in terms of the four quadrants shown in Figure 5.1. Before Dave approached Max with his new idea, their relationship, while a good one, was transactional. From Dave's perspective, the space he was leasing, in and of itself, did not directly have an impact on one of his core business processes; and the rhythm of the relationship was non-intensive as Dave had limited interactions with Max other than sending in his rent, thereby expending limited resources.

However, by approaching Max with a new value proposition, one in which they both realize increased value, Dave and Max are transforming their relationship into a collaborative one: a relationship that has a direct impact on one or more of the three

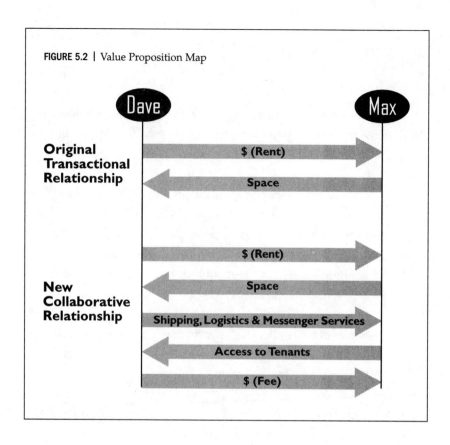

FIGURE 5.2 | Value Proposition Map

Dave   **Max**

Original Transactional Relationship

$ (Rent)

Space

New Collaborative Relationship

$ (Rent)

Space

Shipping, Logistics & Messenger Services

Access to Tenants

$ (Fee)

core business processes. In Dave's case, the new understanding with Max results in access to potential customers (the tenants), thereby having an impact on his customer acquisition and retention process. At the same time, the new value proposition adds to Max's product and service offerings (discounts and special services) that are made available to his tenants and that Max hopes will ultimately have an impact on his customer retention. And if all goes well, Max will start earning fees from Dave.

We hope this simple example gives you a better understanding of the type of process you go through to move a relationship from a transactional relationship to a collaborative one. In the next chapter, we'll focus on how you can shift your relationships, interaction after interaction, iteration after iteration, into a more desirable quadrant.

WHAT HAVE WE LEARNED?

1 ▋ The objective of purposeful collaboration is to create a win-win relationship while engaging in activities that satisfy both parties' customers and build a profitable business.

2 ▋ Start by analyzing *every* business relationship with respect to (1) the *nature* of the relationship and (2) the *rhythm* of the relationship. We use these two perspectives because the nature of the relationship provides an indication of how important a relationship is for achieving your goals, whereas the rhythm of the relationship gives you a sense of your commitment of resources to that relationship.

3 ▋ The nature of the relationship refers to whether you are receiving currencies from a relationship that help you achieve your goals. If you are, then that relationship is core.

4 ▋ Non-core relationships are all those other relationships you have that play a supporting role in your business but don't relate directly to achieving your goals.

5 ▋ When identifying your goals, make sure every goal passes the "S-M-A-R-T" test—that is, each goal is **S**pecific, **M**easurable, **A**ttainable, **R**elevant, and **T**ime sensitive.

6 ▋ Customer relationships can be non-core if the only exchange of value is their payment to you for your product and service and your fulfilling and servicing their needs in the normal daily course of your business.

7 ▋ The *rhythm* of a relationship relates to the patterned flow and intensity of the interactions between you and the other party.

8 ▌ Collaboration requires strong and trusting relationships, which require an intensive rhythm of the relationship.

9 ▌ A relationship has value, even if cash doesn't change hands, if it helps you more quickly and less expensively validate or invalidate the critical assumptions you've made about how you intend to achieve your goals.

10 ▌ A transactional relationship is a non-core relationship that has a non-intensive rhythm.

11 ▌ A relationship characterized as a resource sink is one in which the value accruing to you from the relationship is not core but has an intensive rhythm.

12 ▌ A relationship characterized as a resource opportunity provides core value even though the rhythm of your interaction with the other party is non-intensive, thus not requiring you to use a lot of your resources.

13 ▌ A collaborative relationship is one in which the other party provides core value to you and you provide core value to it. And reflective of the value accruing to both, the rhythm of the relationship is intensive.

14 ▌ Never forget that achieving and maintaining success in business is a never-ending, iterative process.

15 ▌ The ability to identify the most important relationships and then bring to those relationships a continuous stream of value propositions that produce increasing value for each party is what is important. And integral to enhancing those value propositions is the understanding and systematic use of cash and non-cash currencies as well as a method of valuing, measuring, and managing the utility of those currencies.

CHAPTER 6

Deciding Who to Dance With

The last chapter introduced the Relationship Matrix as a way of looking at business relationships and assigning them to one of four quadrants based on the nature and the rhythm of the relationship. The benefit of this approach is that it enables you to categorize all of your relationships in terms of their ability to provide you with strategic and financial value.

At the same time, each of the four relationship quadrants also reflects the resources you are committing to a relationship relative to the currencies offered to you. Ideally, the perceived value of the currencies you receive should influence the rhythm of the relationship and help you decide the future level of resources you commit to that relationship. Because this is most likely the first time you have systematically surveyed the linkage between the utility of the currencies you are receiving and the resources you are committing, you probably have a number of business relationships that are out of balance, in that you are committing too many or too few resources. However, while it is inevitable that some relationships will always be out of balance (and some for good reason), it is obviously extremely important to ensure that the total of the currencies you receive from your network of relationships provides what you need to accomplish your goals.

An additional complexity of business relationships is that every interaction you have with an individual can lead to a change in the currencies that relationship brings. Such change should also lead to a diminution or increase in the intensity of relationships. For example, you may learn from a meeting with someone that she has just changed jobs, as a result of which she is now able to bring different currencies to your relationship. In view of the fact that the currencies she can now bring may either add to or reduce her value to you, your own level of resource commitment to her may warrant a change. Of course, these changes can work in reverse. As your currencies change over time, those changes alter the value you bring to your relationships, leading, perhaps, to a change in the currencies others provide you.

We know that this all sounds very cold and calculating. After all, relationships are between people and yet we don't seem to be factoring into the process the human aspects of relationships. And to be perfectly honest, to some extent you're right. But even though all business relationships are processed through human beings, the purpose of the Relationship Matrix is to momentarily take the human element out of the relationship and allow you to analyze the business value of your relationships. Such an analysis is vital to the success of your business, particularly in an age when collaboration is essential. Our analysis is not about friendship; it is about how best to allocate your energy and resources throughout your business day. This allocation is a business decision, and business decisions should be made on the basis of what is good for your business.

▌ **The Relationship Matrix takes the** human element out and allows you to analyze the utility of your relationships relative to your goals.

Our intent is to demonstrate the benefit of using Purposeful Collaboration to allocate your resources. Let's consider a simple example. Perhaps you've been asked to meet with someone to network, and although you may have wanted to help, you felt that given your existing commitments, you had no alternative other than to say, "I'm sorry, I just don't have the time right now." But let's be honest; we all know that what you *really* meant was that the meeting wasn't important enough for you to reshuffle your tight schedule. In other words, you were allocating your resources but on the fly and without much analysis.

The problem is that your schedule may be filled with a number of things that are not important. And because you're most likely not systematically assessing the value of what you receive from your relationships, you're thus unable to take advantage of more important opportunities. In contrast, by using the Relationship Matrix, you can engage in Purposeful Collaboration with your network of relationships and allocate your resources to those that provide you the most value *and* leave you time to take advantage of other opportunities as they come along.

We are not saying that every relationship has to be managed by the dictates of the Relationship Matrix. Let's look at another example to see what we mean. Let's say you have a vendor that you've dealt with for a long time. And let's say further that this vendor was the first to offer your company credit; and the owner gave you some good business advice along the way. Now, however, the owner is a year from retirement and hasn't kept his business as up-to-date as he should have, and when you look at your relationship via the matrix, you see that his company is a borderline resource sink. His supplies are often late and sometimes wrong. However, you know your company is now an important customer, so you decide to stick with him for the next year, and then if the new owner doesn't modernize, you'll find a new supplier. Your decision, of course, is not made according to the standards of the Relationship Matrix. In this case, it's done with your feelings of loyalty, but it's also done with your eyes wide open. You've analyzed the situation, know the pluses and minuses, and made your decision. You are still managing the relationship. You are still in control, even though the decision was made more with your heart than your wallet.

ITERATING A RELATIONSHIP

In the previous chapter we talked about how our friend Dave went about changing the nature of his relationship with his landlord, Max, from one that was transactional to one that was collaborative. We also demonstrated that changing the relationship was a process. After Dave demonstrated to Max the opportunity to derive mutual strategic benefit by iterating their relationship, Max committed a few resources (printing flyers). If Max's tenants responded, Dave would offer discounted services and then begin to pay Max. Who knows where the relationship could go from there. But what we do know is that it takes a number of interactions for Dave and Max to iterate their relationship to the desired category. And, of course, both Dave and Max are aware that the value proposition underlying their new collaborative relationship will continue to change over time, iteration after iteration, as their respective goals and currencies change.

But if you stand back from the details, what we really see taking place is an example of trading in relationship currencies. When Dave decides to approach Max about offering his services to Max's tenants, essentially Dave is envisioning where their relationship can go and then setting about bringing that vision to fruition.

Let's take a closer look at the process Dave is using to transform the relationship. Dave asks himself two questions about the current status of his relationship with Max:

1. Is Max currently assisting me in achieving any of my important goals?

2. Is my relationship with Max intensive?

As we know, the answer to both questions is no. But Dave doesn't stop there. He then asks two additional questions:

3. Could Max assist me in achieving my goals by providing any currencies that I need?

4. Could I give Max any currencies that will help him achieve his goals?

Again, as we know, this time Dave answers both of these questions with a yes. As the story unfolds, we see that Dave and Max reach a new value proposition in which both receive a currency from the other that they were not previously receiving. Dave gets access to potential customers (Max's tenants) and Max offers additional services to his tenants (Dave's shipping and logistics services as well as Myer's messenger service), thus generating an additional revenue stream.

Now that we understand the steps Dave followed to iterate his relationship with Max, let's take a look at the process in a more general sense.

FOUR QUESTIONS

If we start with the four questions that Dave asked himself relative to his relationship with Max, we can then reword them to work for all of your relationships:

Current Relationship Assessment

1. Is this person currently assisting me in achieving any of my goals by providing me with currencies that add strategic value?

2. Is the rhythm of this relationship intensive?

Future Relationship Assessment

3. Could this person provide me with currencies that add strategic value by helping me achieve any of my goals?

4. Could I offer currencies to this person that will help this person achieve his or her goals?

As you can see, just as Dave did in his relationship with Max, we have two questions that assess the current state of the relationship and two additional questions that envision how potential currencies offered or received can change the relationship. By answering these four questions about every business relationship and using the grid in Figure 6.1, you can segment your relationships into one of the nine different relationship scenario categories shown.

■ **Answering four questions about every** business relationship segments them into one of nine different relationship scenario categories.

In developing these relationship scenarios, we made the underlying assumption that we will only consider options that move relationships up and to the right. Unless you are trying to move a relationship from a resource sink to the transactional category and thereby free up time, energy, and currencies, we assume that you will derive greater value from moving a relationship from non-core to core and from non-intensive to intensive. We also assume that an intensive relationship remains intensive unless you take specific action to change the level of intensity. Given these assumptions, if your answer to question 1 is "Yes," then the answer to question 3 will be "Yes." Also, if your answer to question 2 is "Yes," then the answer to question 4 will be "Yes." Consequently, Figures 6.1 and 6.2 show the nine scenarios on which to focus

FIGURE 6.1 | The Four Questions

Question 1 Does this person currently provide me with a currency? Yes/No	Question 2 Is the relationship intensive? Yes/No	Question 3 Could this person provide me with a currency? Yes/No	Question 4 Could I provide a currency of value to the other person? Yes/No	Scenario Category	Scenario Name
Yes	Yes	Yes	Yes	A	Collaborative Relationship
No	Yes	Yes	Yes	B	Critical Collaborative Opportunity
No	No	Yes	Yes	C	Potential Collaborative Opportunity
Yes	No	Yes	Yes	D	Collaborative Opportunity
Yes	No	Yes	No	E	Resource Opportunity
No	No	Yes	No	F	Long Shot
No	Yes	No	Yes	G	Resource Sink
No	No	No	Yes	H	Potential Resource Sink
No	No	No	No	I	Transactional Relationship

based on these assumptions, as opposed to all 16 possible combinations of Yes/No answers to the four questions.

ALTERNATIVE SCENARIOS

As you can see in Figure 6.2, given our assumptions, these four questions result in defining the two different types of relationship scenarios represented on the matrix by either an arrow or an asterisk. First, let's look at the four scenarios denoted with an asterisk and a letter: *A, *E, *G, and *I. These four scenarios represent relationships for which the *current* quadrant and *future* quadrant are the same. They are relationships that do not move to another quadrant because you cannot identify a change in the

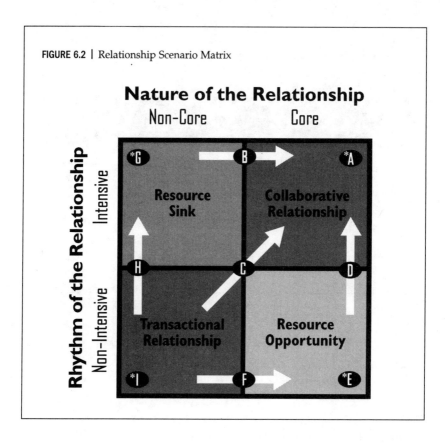

FIGURE 6.2 | Relationship Scenario Matrix

currencies you are currently giving or receiving. For example, *E denotes a relationship that is currently a resource opportunity and for which its future state is also a resource opportunity because you haven't yet figured out a way to take advantage of the opportunity or you are not yet in the position to commit the resources necessary to take advantage of the opportunity. In addition to the four scenarios that stay in the same category, five relationship scenarios are represented by arrows. These scenarios represent relationships that have the potential to move from one relationship category to another based on your answers to questions 3 and 4. For example, Scenario B represents a relationship that is currently a resource sink but has the potential over time to move to a collaborative relationship. Again, it is important to stress that it may take a number of iterations to move a relationship from its current category to its future category.

We'll talk more about how relationships iterate over time after we take a closer look at what each of these nine relationship scenarios means:

Scenario A: Collaborative Relationship. A relationship that has a continuous bidirectional flow of currencies of core value to both parties. Again, collaborative relationships are built over time and are based on trust and mutual benefit.

Scenario B: Critical Collaborative Opportunity. A relationship that, although currently a resource sink, has the potential to iterate into a collaborative relationship. However, if you do not see the possibility of receiving currencies of core value in a reasonable time, reduce your resource commitment and thereby move the relationship into the transactional quadrant.

Scenario C: Potential Collaborative Opportunity. A transactional relationship you believe can and should iterate into a mutually beneficial collaborative relationship. Remember that some relationships work better at the transactional level so you don't have to turn all transactional relationships into collaborative ones.

Scenario D: Collaborative Opportunity. A relationship that starts as a resource opportunity but has the potential to move to collaboration. In this scenario, you see an opportunity to provide currencies of core value to the other party, thereby allowing you to continue to receive currencies of core value to you.

Scenario E: Resource Opportunity. A current relationship you see remaining as a resource opportunity. However, remember that a resource opportunity relationship is not a viable long-term situation because of the unbalanced nature (win-lose) of the current value proposition. Unless you turn it into a collaborative relationship, you may lose the currencies you are receiving from the other party.

Scenario F: Long Shot. A relationship that starts as a transactional one but has the potential to become a resource opportunity as you believe you can receive currencies of core value. However, a resource opportunity is not a viable long-term relationship because of the win-lose value proposition, so you must decide what you can give as well as receive to establish a core relationship.

Scenario G: Resource Sink. A relationship that you expect will remain a resource sink. Even though resource sink relationships consume a lot of your resources as a result of the intensive nature of their rhythm, they do not provide you with currencies of core value. Consequently, if you cannot raise the value of the currencies you are receiving, you should reduce your resource commitment and move the relationship into the transactional quadrant.

Scenario H: Potential Resource Sink. A relationship that is moving from the transactional to the resource sink quadrant, which may not be a desirable change given the resulting drain on resources. As such, you need to be very purposeful before allowing any of your relationships to become resource sinks.

Scenario I: Transactional Relationship. A relationship that is, and will continue to be, transactional. Transactional relationships are a viable state and for many relationships are exactly suited to their purpose because they consume so few resources.

THE RELATIONSHIP DANCE

Throughout this chapter we have talked about moving relationships from one relationship quadrant to a more desirable quadrant, as Dave did with Max. We have also said that it will most often take you several interactions before your relationship reaches the desired new category. And although the arrows in Figure 6.2 are drawn as straight lines, it is more likely that the interaction-by-interaction "dance" between you and the other party will *not* follow a straight line.

> ∎ **The interaction-by-interaction dance** will *not* follow a straight line as the relationship iterates to a more desirable scenario.

Let's go back to the Dave and Max example. If you recall, Dave took the lead by approaching Max with his concept of how they might provide additional benefit (currencies) to each other. That is, Dave first offered his services to Max's tenants, so Dave provided his currency before Max responded in kind. Max could have learned from Dave and then taken Dave's ideas to another vendor. Because Dave offered his currency first, the actual path their dance took wasn't a direct line from transactional to collaborative as reflected by arrow C. In reality, the relationship followed the path (transactional–resource sink–collaborative) as shown in Figure 6.3a. On the other hand, had Max been the one to offer additional currencies first, from Dave's perspective the dance would have followed the path (transactional–resource opportunity–collaborative) as shown in Figure 6.3b.

Why is the path of the dance important?

The path a relationship follows as it iterates is important because, as we've already mentioned and will discuss in greater detail in the next chapter, the location of a relationship on the Relationship Matrix is time dependent. Looking at any relationship periodically or, even better, after every interaction will most likely reveal changes in currencies given or received and changes in what each party considers to be of strategic value. Consequently, if Dave (or his silent partner or backer) performed an audit of his relationships and saw his relationship with Max was in the resource sink category at that point, he might reduce

FIGURE 6.3 | Relationship Iteration

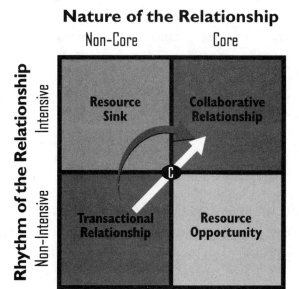

Figure 6.3a

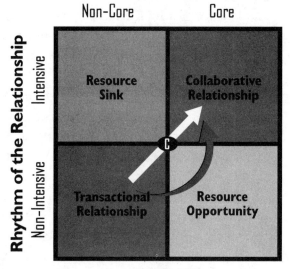

Figure 6.3b

the intensity of the rhythm of the relationship (diverting resources away from Max) unless the objective of the relationship was understood; and thus the relationship would not iterate to the desired collaborative relationship category. However, Dave knows what he is trying to accomplish by first moving into the resource-sink category on his way to a collaborative relationship, so he will pay close attention to the progress being made because he doesn't want the relationship to remain a resource sink.

Note that most relationships you are trying to develop will spend some time as resource sinks because cultivating a relationship does take time and other resources. A typical example is a salesperson wooing a potential customer. That prospect will fall into the resource sink category until a sale is made.

PRIORITIZING YOUR DANCE CARD

Now that we've discussed all of the elements of the Relationship Scenario Matrix, let's shift focus and look at how to use the matrix to determine the specific relationships to which you will allocate your resources.

Step 1: Identify your goals. The first thing to do is write down the S-M-A-R-T goals (described in Chapter 5) you are trying to achieve in the current period by using a form like that shown in Figure 6.4, the Goal-Weighting Table. Although we've only shown space for four goals, you can have as many as you feel are necessary. However, we recommend that you limit your number of goals in any given period to three or four so you can focus your resources on what's most important to you at that moment.

Step 2: Weight each goal. Because it is likely that some of your goals are more important than others, you should assign a percentage-weighting factor to each goal. As seen in Figure 6.4, the *total* weighting for all of your goals must equal 100 percent. If you don't want to assign a specific weight to each goal, then

FIGURE 6.4 | Goal-Weighting Table

Goal Number	Description of Goal	Goal Weighting 100%
1		
2		
3		
4		

all goals are assumed to be of equal importance to you. Keep in mind there is no "right" answer for how much weight should be assigned to any given goal. What matters is the relative weighting of each goal.

Step 3: Identify currencies needed. Using Figure 6.5, the Currency/Goal Linkage Table, identify the currencies you need to realize each of your goals by checking the respective boxes under each goal. In the next chapter we'll walk you through a detailed example of how to identify the specific currencies you need to achieve a goal.

Step 4: Answer the four questions. Now, systematically answer each of the four questions for every one of your relation-

FIGURE 6.5 | Currency/Goal Linkage Table

Currencies \ Goals	Goal 1	Goal 2	Goal 3	Goal 4
Cash				
Customers				
Products and Services				
Competencies				
Validation				
Technology				
Intellectual Property				
Other				

ships in your database, even if your database consists of 350 business cards held together by an elastic band. To get started, use Figure 6.6, My Relationships, and refer back to Figure 6.1 (The Four Questions) to identify the scenario category each of your relationships falls into. By doing this, you can sort your relationships into the nine scenario categories shown in Figure 6.2.

After performing this task, let's assume your 350 names are sorted as follows:

Scenario A: Collaborative Relationship	3
Scenario B: Critical Collaborative Opportunity	8
Scenario C: Potential Collaborative Opportunity	31
Scenario D: Collaborative Opportunity	8
Scenario E: Resource Opportunity	7
Scenario F: Long Shot	33
Scenario G: Resource Sink	15
Scenario H: Potential Resource Sink	25
Scenario I: Transactional Relationship	220
TOTAL	**350**

(Scenarios A–D } 50)

FIGURE 6.6 | My Relationships

Name	Question 1 Does this person currently provide me with a currency? Yes/No	Question 2 Is the relationship intensive? Yes/No	Question 3 Could this person provide me with a currency? Yes/No	Question 4 Could I provide a currency of value to the other person? Yes/No	Scenario Category

Step 5: Prioritize scenario categories. Recalling our discussion of what it means to have a relationship in any given scenario, you know that some scenarios are clearly more important than others. Deciding which scenarios to look at first, however, is clearly a personal decision. Nonetheless, it is helpful in setting priorities to look at the scenarios in major groupings. Scenarios A–D can be thought of as builders, in that these relationships either already are, or (you believe) can become, collaborative relationships. Scenarios E and F are longer shots in that you still have to identify the currencies that will transform those relationships into collaborative ones. The relationships in Scenario G obviously need attention as it is there you can free up resources to use for your relationships in Scenarios A–D. And, as we mentioned, you clearly do not want to allocate any additional resources to rela-

tionships in Scenario H. Last, we arrive at the largest category, Scenario I, which is made up of our transactional relationships that are most likely OK where they are.

Clearly, by using the four questions you can now categorize your relationships and then, depending on your specific situation, decide how many of the nine scenarios, and in which order, to focus on in greater detail.

Given the above distribution, a total of 50 relationships exist in Scenarios A–D that require a much more detailed look because of their current and future value. In the next chapter, we'll turn our attention to how we accomplish that.

WHAT HAVE WE LEARNED?

1 ∎ The perceived value of the currencies you receive should influence the rhythm of a relationship and help you decide the future level of resources you commit to that relationship.

2 ∎ An additional complexity of business relationships is that every interaction you have can lead to a change in the currencies that a particular relationship brings. This change should also lead to a diminution or increase in the intensity of that relationship.

3 ∎ The purpose of the Relationship Matrix is to momentarily take the human element out of relationships and allow you to analyze the business value of your relationships.

4 ∎ By using the Relationship Matrix, you have the ability to trade in relationship currencies with your network of relationships and allocate your resources to those relationships that provide you the most value.

5 ▌ The four questions to ask yourself for all of your relationships are:

Current Relationship Assessment

1. Is this person currently assisting me in achieving any of my goals by providing me with currencies that add strategic value?

2. Is the rhythm of this relationship intensive?

Future Relationship Assessment

3. Could this person provide me with currencies that add strategic value by helping me achieve any of my goals?

4. Could I offer currencies to this person that will help him/her achieve his/her goals?

6 ▌ By answering the four questions about every business relationship and using the grid in Figure 6.1, you can segment your relationships into one of the nine different relationship scenario categories shown.

7 ▌ It will most often take you several interactions to move to a more desirable quadrant, and it is likely that the interaction-by-interaction "dance" between you and the other party will not follow a straight line.

8 ▌ Looking at any relationship from month to month or after every interaction will most likely reveal changes in currencies given or received and changes in what each party considers to be of strategic value.

9 ▌ The first thing to do is write down the S-M-A-R-T goals you want to achieve and assign a weighting factor to each goal, because at any one time some of your goals most likely are more important than others.

10 ▌ Then identify the currencies you need to realize your goals.

11 ▌ Now, systematically answer each of the four questions for every one of your relationships to identify the scenario category each of your relationships falls into.

CHAPTER 7

Measuring the Value of Every Relationship

As a choreographer, you build your Collaborative Community around a defining set of customers' needs and wants. And you also build your Collaborative Community one relationship at a time, following a process of value proposition enhancement much like the one Dave used in his dealings with Max. But now that you've assessed which relationships deserve the commitment of your time and other resources, how do you assess your overall progress? That is, because you are involved in interacting with many relationships at the same time, how do you assess whether these interactions are resulting in a gain in value toward achieving your goals?

This question is important because the intent of Purposeful Collaboration is to help you allocate your limited resources to those relationships that provide you the most value. Again referring back to our example, Dave wanted to gain access to Max's tenants because he believed he could convert those tenants into customers, thereby validating his assumption that commercial property managers could serve as a distribution channel for his shipping and logistics services.

▌**Purposeful Collaboration helps you allocate** your limited resources to those relationships that provide the greatest value.

However, collaborative relationships are not very easily measured, so in order to assess whether interacting with any given relationship results in a gain, you have to determine the value of the currencies used in the value proposition between the other party and yourself. But how? Should you try to convert the non-cash currencies into their estimated dollar equivalency or should you try to convert all currencies, including cash, into a numeric value?

VALUING RELATIONSHIP CURRENCIES

It is our view that attempting to calculate the cash equivalency of non-cash currencies is extremely difficult. How can you assess the dollar value of an introduction to someone who has a particular technology you need? You really can't do it with any degree of confidence. But what you *can* do is assess whether that currency, the introduction to the person with the technology, is of high, medium, or low utility in helping you achieve your goals. The utility value you assess is determined by such factors as the likelihood you will obtain and utilize the currency within the time frame you've set for achieving your goals, the magnitude of the currency, and the intensity of interactions (which reflects the commitment of your resources) required to obtain the currency.

In addition, you have to distinguish between the three currency levels we discussed in Chapter 4: information about, access to, or actual currency. Thus, in the above instance you were given access to the person who has the technology.

When you put these two scales together—the utility of the currency and the level of the currency—you have the ability to value what you receive in relation to the goals you are trying to achieve. To do this, locate the intersection of the utility-currency-level scales on the Value-Rating Table (Figure 7.1), where we have used a relatively simple 5-point rating system to assign a numeric value to the currency.

■ **A 5-point rating system** assigns a numeric value to the currency based on the intersection of the utility ranking and currency level.

We have shaded the utility scale and represented the currency levels by shapes to more easily keep track of why you selected a specific value rating. Because the table has two cells with a value of 2, three cells with a value of 3, and two cells with a value of 4, the shading and shapes help track whether you chose, for example, a value of 2 because the currency you could receive was "access to/low utility" or "information about/medium utility."

We realize the Value Rating Table is subjective. Then again, many important aspects of business are inherently subjective.

FIGURE 7.1 | Value-Rating Table

	Currency Level		
Utility	Information About	Access To	Actual Currency
Low	1	2	3
Medium	2	3	4
High	3	4	5

For example, generally accepted accounting principles contain subjective concepts like valuing inventory or accounts receivable reserves or estimating future warranty costs. But even though subjectivity is involved, we believe that if the subjectivity is consistently applied within a static framework, it allows an objective measurement. Plus, as you gain experience in valuing currencies, the extent of the subjectivity you introduce into the process diminishes.

For instance, referring back to Dave and Max, let's look at how Dave might assign a currency level/utility value to the currency he believes Max offers. Given Dave's belief in the high utility of his access to Max's 300 tenants, when Max's flyer advertising the new service hits the mail, Dave might assign a 4 to that currency. But as Dave gains experience in his ability to convert Max's tenants into customers, he'll develop a better understanding of how many of the 300 tenants he's likely to gain. Thus, the value rating may change over time. If in Dave's actual experience the number of tenants he converts turns out to be smaller than he expected, he may lower the utility ranking to medium or even low, which will result in a change in value from a 4 to a 3, or perhaps even a 2. If he gains more tenants as customers, he may conclude that Max doesn't just offer him access to customers but actual customers, because Max's customers sign up without a further sales effort. In this instance, Dave might raise the value rating to a 5, representing a high value/actual currency.

THE RELATIONSHIP SCORECARD

Using this value rating system combined with your goals, you can measure the value you are receiving, or could receive, from every currency in every relationship. In Figure 7.2, we have developed a Relationship Scorecard to help you determine, and account for, both the value of every relationship at a specific point in time (the current state) and the value you believe it

FIGURE 7.2 | Relationship Scorecard

Name:		Date:		
Goal Weighting (100%)	__%	__%	__%	__%
Currencies ⟍ Goals	Goal 1	Goal 2	Goal 3	Goal 4
Cash				
Customers				
Products and Services				
Competencies				
Validation				
Technology				
Intellectual Property				
Other				
Weighted Totals				
Relationship Value (RV)				

could offer within the time frame you've set for achieving your goals (the future state).

Thus, in using the Relationship Scorecard, you need to create two separate scorecards for every relationship. The first scorecard calculates the current value; the second one calculates the future value. It represents what you believe you could receive if you struck a value proposition or series of value propositions that mines all the possible currencies that relationship offers relative to the goals you've set. Remember that just because someone has currencies that could benefit you, he or she is not going to offer them unless the required trust exists and you identify currencies you have that the other person wants. That's the work involved in building the value propositions that underlie win-win relationships. In building collaborative relationships, you have to give to get.

Right about now, you may be thinking this looks like too much work. But don't forget, by using the four questions from Chapter 6, we've already filtered your relationships from a total of 350 down to 50. What the Relationship Scorecard does is allow you to more carefully prioritize and focus on those 50 relationships. And to be honest, it does take some time the first time you go through the process. But once you are more familiar with the process, it simply becomes part of the way you work. Because much of the labor consists of updating ongoing relationships, the effort is not as arduous as you might imagine, particularly considering the benefits. (For information on our easy and inexpensive software tool called RelationsWeb that categorizes the relationships and performs the calculations for you, visit <www.relationsweb.com>.)

Now let's take a more detailed look at the Relationship Scorecard, which is structured to link the specific currencies you receive, or could receive, to specific goals. In addition, the scorecard encompasses the weighting factor you've assigned to each goal as discussed in Chapter 6. And although we've shown only four goal columns, you can use as many as you need. However, we believe that in establishing goals, it is better to limit the number of goals to three or four S-M-A-R-T goals as adding more goals makes it harder to focus on what's most important to you. The goals you establish should be for whatever objectives you pursue within a specified time frame.

Consequently, whether you are a free agent or a corporate executive, you can tailor the Relationship Scorecard to help you identify what is most important to you and your business. We believe that what is most important always relates to the three core business processes: (1) how you get and keep your customers, (2) how you develop the products and services that satisfy the customers' needs, and (3) how you deliver to and service your customers.

The currencies we've identified (six non-cash and cash) are the same ones we first discussed in Chapter 4. Again, the six non-cash relationship currencies are:

1. *Customers*—People who buy your primary product or service

2. *Products and services*—Another party's primary product or service you make use of in achieving your goals

3. *Competencies*—People-embodied skills necessary for your community to function effectively

4. *Validation*—A testimonial to the value you offer or in support of your expertise

5. *Technology*—A manner of accomplishing a task, especially technical processes, methods, or knowledge

6. *Intellectual property*—Proprietary know-how

The non-cash categories listed above cover the currencies most often used in the value propositions that underlie customer-centric, collaborative businesses. However, your job is to tailor this list to the specific currencies you believe important to obtain and utilize in pursuit of your goals.

Suppose all your goals are related to developing a new product for your company, and you identify cash, competencies, and intellectual property as the currencies you require. The inherent flexibility of the scorecard allows you to better define the two non-cash currencies. For instance, suppose the competencies you need at this early stage are the ability to model concepts in your collaborative product design environment and get potential customers to try the product. List these more finely defined currencies on the scorecard. Or dig even deeper. The scorecard provides the framework for you to define both your goals and the currencies you think are required for achieving your goals as finely as you choose to "slice and dice" them. And if you use a currency category other than those we have identified, simply substitute your currency under the box labeled "Other" on the scorecard.

▌ The scorecard provides the framework to define your goals and the currencies required for achieving them.

The final components of the Relationship Scorecard are the Weighted Totals and the Relationship Value (RV). The Weighted Totals are the calculated values of the currency values based on the weighting you've placed on each goal. This number is determined by multiplying the weighting you assign to each goal by the corresponding currency value(s) in that goal's column. The Relationship Value is the sum of the weighted totals of all of your goals. In the next section we'll demonstrate the calculation utilizing a comprehensive example to see how the Relationship Scorecard measures the value in your relationships.

USING THE PROCESS

Assume for a moment that you've just been awarded a partnership in a successful CPA firm. Together with your partners, you agree that your primary focus is to meet the firm's overall goals for customer acquisition and retention. Thus, you set the following specific goals and weights for yourself for the coming year (Figure 7.3). Next, you identify the currencies (regardless of level) you require to achieve your goals. That is, you think about your goals broadly and brainstorm about the types of currencies you believe will assist you in achieving your goals. You also think about when you need access to the currency and when you'll need the ability to use or trade it. The element of

FIGURE 7.3 | Your Weighted Goals

Goal Number	Description of Goal	Goal Weighting 100%
1	Sign up 5 business clients who require business planning, audit, and tax services.	35
2	Sign up 20 personal clients who want you to help with their financial planning.	15
3	Sign up 10 business clients for your new financial information systems design practice.	30
4	Maintain the firm's five-year running average customer retention rate of 90%, while reducing communication costs by 10%.	20

time is important because if you can't get and use a currency in the time frame you've established, the value of the currency could be diminished. Now that you have a method to record and track currencies, you'll know that some are already "in your bank," such as the proprietary know-how related to your position or the resources of friends and associates you can count on. Others, you will need to find. Once you've thought about all these items, check off the currencies you need to find in your Currency/Goal Linkage Table (Figure 7.4).

If you think that using relationship currencies is a novel concept, consider for a minute the term *bootstrapping*, which is what entrepreneurs do when unable to raise all the money they need to start and grow their business (an all-too-common occur-

FIGURE 7.4 | Your Currency/Goal Linkage Table

Currencies \ Goals	Goal 1	Goal 2	Goal 3	Goal 4
Cash	✓	✓	✓	
Customers	✓	✓	✓	
Products and Services	✓	✓	✓	✓
Competencies	✓	✓	✓	✓
Validation	✓	✓	✓	
Technology				✓
Intellectual Property				
Other				

rence). *Webster's Dictionary* defines bootstrapping as "promoting or developing by initiative and effort with little or no assistance." And that's essentially what we're talking about: creatively devising how to parlay non-cash currencies into what you need to achieve your goals. In a corporate setting this is often referred to as "leveraging assets." In other words, you're trying to use what you have and gain access to what you need but don't have. Either way, you're bootstrapping.

Now that you know the currencies you need, assume that the filtering of the 350 names we discussed in Chapter 6 is based on the goals you identified in Figure 7.3. In our example, this filtering resulted in 50 Scenario A–D relationships. The next step is to analyze the currencies each of these relationships offers relative to the currencies required to achieve your goals. Let's examine the process in detail for just a few of these 50 relationships.

Sharon Smith. You've done Sharon Smith's tax return for three years. During the past year you've helped her with some financial planning decisions as she quickly rose to become a vice president at one of the largest advertising and public relations firms in the city. But advertising has been significantly affected by the downturn in the economy and Sharon was recently laid off. For Sharon, this turn of events represents the opportunity to become the choreographer of her own business. She comes to you because she needs your expertise and also because you have lots of customers she hopes can become her customers. She doesn't have a lot of money, but she has thought about your business, the manner in which you communicate with customers, and how she can help you do so more effectively. She hopes she'll soon have lots of customers that can become your customers, and she wants to work out a trade. What do you do? You answer the four questions for Sharon as shown in Figure 7.5. Referring back to Figure 6.1 (The Four Questions), you conclude that Sharon fits into Relationship Scenario C—Potential Collaborative Opportunity.

Len Collins. Len is a senior vice president in the largest bank in your city, and his brother is managing director of an important venture capital firm. You and Len meet for lunch once or twice a year, run into each other at networking events, and occasionally get together in a foursome during charity golf outings. Len always

FIGURE 7.5 | Evaluating Relationships

Name	Question 1 Does this person currently provide me with a currency? Yes/No	Question 2 Is the relationship intensive? Yes/No	Question 3 Could this person provide me with a currency? Yes/No	Question 4 Could I provide a currency of value to the other person? Yes/No	Scenario Category
Sharon Smith	N	N	Y	Y	C
Len Collins	Y	N	Y	Y	D
Stephen White	N	Y	Y	Y	B

makes it a point to introduce you to the people he knows on these occasions, and several have become personal tax clients. However, he hasn't referred any of his business customers to you, nor can you really think of anyone you've introduced to him that has become a customer of his bank. You believe your recent promotion to partner will change that. Again, what do you do? You enter your answers to the four questions for Len in Figure 7.5, concluding that he fits into Relationship Scenario D—Collaborative Opportunity.

Stephen White. You and Stephen serve together on the board of a local not-for-profit. He is a very successful condominium developer who buys up and renovates older buildings in city neighborhoods. Because, like politics, real estate is local, Stephen is very well connected to city government, local financial institutions, and the media as well as to prominent members of the community. You're currently doing the tax work on a few of his developments, but he lowballs you on price. Always one to ask the quick question, Stephen seems to get the information he needs without incurring costs. What do you do? You enter your answers to the four questions for Stephen in Figure 7.5, concluding that Stephen is a Relationship Scenario B—Critical Collaborative Opportunity.

Clearly, each of these people represents an important relationship for someone trying to achieve goals such as yours. But who offers greater value? All have their positives and negatives. Stephen's contacts within local financial institutions may be better than Len's, but Stephen has yet to offer an introduction. Len has access to a circle of people different from Stephen's, including the type of technology companies that will help you achieve Goal 3. Sharon is already a client with access to an entirely different group of possible customers, and her services can benefit your goal of reducing communication costs. Looking at both current and future Relationship Scorecards for each will help answer who is of greater value to you.

DIGGING DEEPER

Let's start with Sharon. Currently, she is a personal tax client, but that relationship is a non-core, transactional one. She is not presently providing you with any currencies to help you achieve your newly assigned goals. Thus, her Current Relationship Value is 0. But you think she could offer you currencies as her business gets going, and you know you can introduce her to the potential customers she wants. To calculate her Future Relationship Value, let's run through the currencies you need and see what your relationship with Sharon can provide. Keep in mind that the future we are referring to is based on your year time frame for achieving your goals:

- *Cash*—She is looking to trade with you and not provide cash.

- *Customers*—Sharon is just starting out, so she doesn't qualify as the type of customer you want under Goal 1. She is already a personal tax client, so she doesn't influence Goal 2. Her financial information system needs are quite simple, so she doesn't represent the customer you are looking for under Goal 3. So you conclude she doesn't fit into the category of any "actual customers" you are presently seeking. Sharon is what we've described as a transactional customer.

  As a plus, Sharon has offered to introduce you to her future customers. You know that in the past she has worked with businesses that would need planning, tax, and audit services, but her contacts are with people in marketing, not finance. So even though she may offer you information about businesses that meet your criteria, you decide to assign her a utility of "Low." Thus, enter a 1 in the Goal 1 column. You really don't see how Sharon can assist with Goal 2, so you skip that column and assess whether she can help you with Goal 3. Here you decide she will, in fact, have access to many companies that fit this category. She plans to work with emerging technology companies that grow quickly, are often backed by venture capital, and thus need good, solid financial information systems. And because with smaller companies she tends to interact with the principals, you rate the utility of her access as "Medium." Thus, enter that value (the 3 representing medium utility/access to) in the Goal 3 column.

- *Products and services*—Instead of giving you cash for your services, Sharon is offering you her services to help your firm become more effective and efficient in communicating with your customers. Because you know the quality of her work and the results she has obtained for some of her customers at her former firm, you decide this actual currency is of medium utility. Thus, you enter that value in the Goal 4 column.

You don't believe Sharon offers any of the other currencies you require, so you calculate the weighted totals thus:

Goal 1: $1 \times .35 = .35$
Goal 2: $0 \times .15 = 0$
Goal 3: $3 \times .30 = .9$
Goal 4: $4 \times .20 = .8$

And then sum the column totals (.35 + 0 + .9 + .8) to get Sharon's Future Relationship Value of 2.05, as shown in Figure 7.6.

Before you make any decisions about Sharon's Relationship Value, move on and complete the scorecards for Len and Stephen. When you think about the currencies Len offers and how they help you achieve your goals, you come to the following conclusions and complete his scorecards accordingly. Many of Len's business customers fit the criteria you've set for Goals 1 and 3, but those aren't the introductions he tends to make. So

FIGURE 7.6 | Sharon Smith's Scorecard

Name: **Sharon Smith**	**Future**		Date: 12/01/02	
Goal Weighting (100%)	**35%**	**15%**	**30%**	**20%**
Currencies ╲ Goals	Goal 1	Goal 2	Goal 3	Goal 4
Cash				
Customers	▲1		●3	
Products and Services				■4
Competencies				
Validation				
Technology				
Intellectual Property				
Other				
Weighted Totals	.35		.9	.8
Relationship Value (RV)	2.05			

Currency Level			
Utility	Information About	Access To	Actual Currency
Low	▲1	●2	■3
Medium	▲2	●3	■4
High	▲3	●4	■5

that currency isn't immediately available. He does give you access to certain individuals who have become personal clients, so you assign a medium value to this access and enter that value in the customer line in the Goal 2 column (Figure 7.7). Although it is nice to be known as a friend of Len's, you don't see how this validation is currently helping you with any of your goals. Next, you recall that you met the tax manager your firm just hired during one of his charity golf events. The tax manager helps you in offering the full services envisioned under Goal 1. You decide this is low value for access and place that value on the competencies line. You total up your scorecard to discover that Len's Current Relationship Value is 1.15.

As you think more about the relationship, you realize that you haven't really offered any of your currencies to Len. Maybe that's why the relationship isn't intensive. You recognize there are many things you can do to bring customers to Len, which you assume is an important goal for him. But just to be clear what you should offer, you look at the currencies you believe Len has available and carefully complete a scorecard for his Future Relationship Value.

As you think about the currencies Len could offer, you determine the following:

- *Customers*—Len can provide you with access to customers across all three of your customer acquisition goals. You know he's well respected, and bankers are generally good referral sources for accountants, so across Goals 1–3, you assess the utility of his access to customers as "High."

- *Products and services*—For the customer base you intend to service, information about sophisticated banking products can be important. Consequently, you decide that Len can offer you information about products and services that has a utility rating of "High."

- *Competencies*—Len's brother is a venture capitalist, and some of the customers you seek will want to obtain this type of financing. Thus, he offers you information about a competency that may help you in attaining customers

FIGURE 7.7 | Len Collins's Scorecards

Name: **Len Collins**	**Current**		Date: 12/01/02	
Goal Weighting (100%)	35%	15%	30%	20%
Currencies \ Goals	Goal 1	Goal 2	Goal 3	Goal 4
Cash				
Customers		3		
Products and Services				
Competencies	2			
Validation				
Technology				
Intellectual Property				
Other				
Weighted Totals	.7	.45		
Relationship Value (RV)	1.15			

Name: **Len Collins**	**Future**		Date: 12/01/02	
Goal Weighting (100%)	35%	15%	30%	20%
Currencies \ Goals	Goal 1	Goal 2	Goal 3	Goal 4
Cash				
Customers	4	4	4	
Products and Services	3	3	3	
Competencies	1		1	
Validation		4		
Technology				
Intellectual Property				
Other				
Weighted Totals	2.8	1.65	2.4	
Relationship Value (RV)	6.85			

Utility	Currency Level		
	Information About	Access To	Actual Currency
Low	1	2	3
Medium	2	3	4
High	3	4	5

who fall under either Goals 1 or 3. You value that utility as "Low," because your relationship is with Len, not with his brother. Of course, you would still have access to the type of contacts that brought your tax manager, but you decide to conservatively value this currency.

- *Validation*—You know Len has offered workshops on financial planning jointly with at least one other CPA firm. If he'd be willing to work with you and your firm to offer such a program, you believe that would provide you with actual validation of your firm's expertise. Len is an important figure in the business community, so you decide that validation would be of medium value in achieving Goal 2; thus you enter a 4 in that cell.

You leave the next three rows blank, recognizing that while Len may offer you information about technology or an introduction to a customer who has information you can use to reduce your communication costs, as per Goal 4, you haven't identified anything specific. Now you calculate the weighted totals (Goal 1: $(4+3+1) \times .35 = 2.8$; Goal 2: $(4+3+4) \times .15 = 1.65$; Goal 3: $(4+3+1) \times .3 = 2.4$) and sum up the scorecard (Figure 7.7) and determine Len's Future Relationship Value is $6.85 = (2.8 + 1.65 + 2.4)$. This validates your intuitive understanding of Len's Future Relationship Value (much greater than Sharon's), but it unnerves you a little. Unless you can offer Len something of value and increase the rhythm of the relationship, his currencies—present and future—may be lost. As we've said, one-way relationships don't last.

Next you turn to Stephen. He certainly isn't one of your favorite customers, as he always seems to have the upper hand and is demanding of your time. However, he's so well connected and successful, it is worth trying to find a way to make this a win-win relationship.

Thinking about the currencies Stephen provides, you realize that in relation to your goals, he offers you none right now.

Even the little bit of cash he pays won't show up on the score-card because, like Sharon, the relationship is non-core. What about Future Value? As you run down the currency list, you determine the following:

- *Cash*—Stephen could be an important client if you can move him from just tax work to the broader array of services on which you wish to focus. In addition, you've seen firsthand that his financial information systems need to be updated. You are fairly confident you can get him started down that path. Consequently, you value the utility of the cash he brings as "Medium."

- *Customers*—He knows everyone in the community and everyone knows him. Certainly Stephen can provide access to potential customers who fall within your target customers. However, as he has never referred anyone to you, this utility is rated as "Low."

- *Validation*—You know that your name will go out to many of Stephen's limited partners as the accountant of record should you get more of his work. That endorsement you value as "High" and believe it relates most directly to Goal 2.

Concluding that these are the total currencies Stephen can provide you, you do the math and come up with a Future Relationship Value (Figure 7.8) for Stephen of 4.95.

In reality, of course, you'd go on to analyze all 50 of your Scenario A–D relationships in a similar manner. You might also take a look at Scenario E and F relationships, recognizing that you probably won't effect any meaningful changes in those at this time. And certainly you'd review your Scenario G relationships to free up resources to focus on Scenario A–D relationships. However, for now, let's just take a look at what we've learned about Sharon, Len, and Stephen.

FIGURE 7.8 | Stephen White's Scorecard

Name: **Stephen White** **Future** Date: 12/01/02				
Goal Weighting (100%)	**35%**	**15%**	**30%**	**20%**
Currencies Goals	Goal 1	Goal 2	Goal 3	Goal 4
Cash	4		4	
Customers	2	2	2	
Products and Services				
Competencies				
Validation		5		
Technology				
Intellectual Property				
Other				
Weighted Totals	2.1	1.05	1.8	
Relationship Value (RV)	4.95			

Utility		Currency Level		
		Information About	Access To	Actual Currency
	Low	1	2	3
	Medium	2	3	4
	High	3	4	5

INTERPRETING THE DATA

To decide on a course of action, you first array Current and Future Relationship values on an Evaluation Grid (Figure 7.9a) and then subtract the Current Relationship Value (CRV) from the Future Relationship Value (FRV). This subtraction (Delta) gives you the numerical equivalent of the value in the relationship you could receive but are not currently benefiting from. Once you've calculated the value in all three relationships, you are then in position to analyze the measurements and decide how to manage each relationship.

> ■ **The Relationship Value Delta provides** the numerical equivalent of the value in the relationship from which you are not currently benefiting.

When you answered the four questions for Sharon, you determined that you and she currently had a transactional relationship, but you thought that perhaps you could—and should—try to iterate the relationship to a collaborative one. However, when you examine the data, you discover that not only does Sharon have the lowest absolute Future Relationship Value of the three but also the smallest Delta and thus the smallest incremental value to be realized.

Stephen is clearly a resource sink, with the potential to be collaborative. Thus you must be careful to closely monitor your continued commitment of resources. If he doesn't begin to give you any of his currencies, you'll want to take the necessary steps to reduce the intensity of the relationship and make it purely transactional. However, there may be a time down the road when you are better able to strike a value proposition that will move the relationship to one that is collaborative.

Len should be your priority. His value is clear, and he has already indicated a willingness to give. Think of his relationship currencies as money on the table. We'll demonstrate in the next chapter how to develop the value propositions and engage in activities that increase the rhythm of a relationship such as Len's so that you can realize the value it offers. If you aren't able to effect this change, you run the risk of losing the relationship.

Accordingly, if you set priorities according to FRV and Delta, you allocate resources first toward building your relationships with Len and Stephen and finally to Sharon. Let's assume for a moment that Len had a CRV of 3.15 instead of 1.15, thus giving him a Delta of 3.70 instead of 5.70 (Figure 7.9b). Although Len would still have the highest Future Value of 6.85 compared with

FIGURE 7.9 | Evaluation Grids

Name	CRV	FRV	DELTA (FRV-CRV)
Sharon Smith	0	2.05	2.05
Len Collins	1.15	6.85	5.70
Stephen White	0	4.95	4.95

Figure 7.9a

Name	CRV	FRV	DELTA (FRV-CRV)
Sharon Smith	0	2.05	2.05
Len Collins	3.15	6.85	3.70
Stephen White	0	4.95	4.95

Figure 7.9b

Stephen's 4.95 and Sharon's 2.05, the highest Delta of 4.95 would belong to Stephen. How would that result change your prioritization? Should you then focus first on Stephen? Probably, but not necessarily. Prioritizing according to the Delta takes into account the totality of the currencies you could receive from that individual. However, you may need to gain access to, and utilize, one currency before another can be effectively used. For example, Stephen's validation will come only after you gain more of his work. Now let's assume the way in which you get more of Stephen's work is by demonstrating to Stephen the validation and access to customers you are getting from Len, the prominent banker. If you need to utilize one individual's currencies before you can realize the value of someone else's currencies, you should take that factor into consideration in your allocation of resources.

You should also consider gaps in the currencies available to you. The Currency/Goal Linkage Table in Figure 7.4 indicates that technology is a necessary currency for the attainment of Goal 4, your customer retention and cost-cutting goal. None of the three relationships we've examined offer technology. If you know you need that currency within 30 days, for example, or otherwise you won't have enough time to achieve your cost-cutting goal, you'll want to focus some of your resources on finding that currency. In this way, identifying and measuring the value in the individual currencies gives you a real-time, predictive metric helpful in assessing progress toward your goals. If on day 30 you still don't have the necessary technology, you know you won't meet that goal based on your original assumptions and plans. Accordingly, you can reevaluate and develop new assumptions and plans based on that knowledge.

While the Relationship Values and Deltas provide an overall indication of value, it is also important to look at the specific currencies relative to your overall situation. So always take some time to step back from the numbers and think about the broader context. Here are a few guidelines that can help you assess your situation and make your decisions:

- Level of effort required in putting together the value proposition that will get you the currencies

- The order in which you need the currencies

- Level of effort to maintain a relationship in its current state

- Ability to use the currency obtained in value propositions with other people

Through this analytic process, had you completed scorecards for all 50 relationships, not only would you know who had the highest relative score, but you'd know where the greatest value for achieving your goals was most likely found. You'd know the specific currencies available to you and where gaps existed that needed to be closed. Thus, you could focus, prioritize, and reduce the risk of spending time and other valuable resources with the wrong people!

Moreover, as you manage your relationships toward the achievement of your goals, you can filter the scorecards any way you see fit. You can quickly prioritize based on who offers you the greatest currencies for Goal 1 as opposed to Goal 4 if at the moment you are working on Goal 1 and not Goal 4. Or you can look at everyone who offers you a particular currency. Although this type of card shuffling takes time, it is still a manageable and powerful tool for realizing the value in your relationships even if you did it manually for 50 people.

Of course, we must bear in mind that just because someone has currencies available doesn't mean you'll receive them or should go after them. For example, you may decide Sharon's relationship should remain transactional and not take her up on her currency offer. More likely, you'll require that she provide her currencies first, thus traversing the path of a transactional-resource opportunity-collaborative relationship. That path is a less risky proposition, as you do not run the danger of her relationship becoming a resource sink. And remember, she approached you, thus signaling her willingness to give in order to get.

VALUE IS IN THE EYES OF THE BEHOLDER

You'll notice we've not attempted to value the currencies *you* bring to a relationship. That's because, as we started Chapter 3 by saying, value is determined in the eyes of the recipient. Only Len can determine if the customer introduction you make is worthy of an exchange. Your job is to treat Len as a customer, which means discovering all you can about his needs and wants and then offering a value proposition built around the currencies you assume he needs and you can offer. Then you learn from each interaction with Len and come back again with a new offer based on your greater level of understanding of his goals and currency needs.

However, even though you cannot value the currencies you provide, you must keep tabs on the currencies you are giving to others. This assists you in making sure you are not overcommitting a specific currency, and it allows you to remember what you've already given to a relationship.

In the next chapter, we'll describe the scope of activity inherent in gaining access to currencies as you build collaborative relationships.

WHAT HAVE WE LEARNED?

1 ▐ The intent of Purposeful Collaboration is to help you allocate your limited resources to those relationships that provide you the most value.

2 ∎ To assess whether interacting with any given relationship results in a gain, you have to determine the value of the currencies used in the value proposition between the other party and yourself.

3 ∎ Assess whether a currency is of high, medium, or low utility in helping you achieve your goals.

4 ∎ Distinguish between the three currency levels we discussed: information about, access to, or actual currency.

5 ∎ A relatively simple 5-point rating system assigns a numeric value to a currency based on the intersection of the utility and currency-level scales.

6 ∎ A Relationship Scorecard helps you determine, and account for, both the value of every relationship at a specific point in time (the current state) and the value you believe it could offer within the time frame you've set for achieving your goals (the future state).

7 ∎ The scorecard gives you the framework to define both your goals and the currencies required for achieving them as finely as you choose to "slice and dice" them.

8 ∎ The scorecard is structured to link the specific currencies you receive, or could receive, to specific goals.

9 ∎ The Relationship Value is the sum of the weighted totals for all of your goals.

10 ∎ To decide on a course of action, you first array Current and Future Relationship Values and then subtract the Current Relationship Value from the Future Relationship Value. This Relationship Value Delta gives you the numerical equivalent of the value in the relationship you could receive but are not currently benefiting from.

11 ▌ Identifying and measuring the value in individual currencies gives you a real-time, predictive metric helpful in assessing progress toward your goals.

12 ▌ We've not attempted to value the currencies you bring to a relationship because value is determined in the eyes of the recipient.

CHAPTER 8

Building Trusting, Purposeful, Win-Win Relationships

We started this book by explaining that success in the era of collaborative business comes from building trusting, purposeful, and mutually beneficial relationships. We've demonstrated how to identify those relationships and how to use both cash and non-cash currencies to expand the value propositions upon which those relationships are based. However, just because someone you know has a currency you need doesn't mean they'll allow you to use it.

So how do you gain access to the currencies you want? The truth is it's not easy. It means engaging in a continuous stream of value propositions that bring each person closer toward his or her respective goals. And as we're sure you know by now, building the kind of win-win, learning relationships required for collaboration takes a great deal of work.

WHO DO YOU TRUST?

Before Johnny Carson went on to fame as the star of *The Tonight Show,* he hosted a television quiz show called *Who Do You Trust?* In and of itself, the program wasn't all that memorable other than for Johnny's quick wit and keen sense of humor. But the title—*Who Do You Trust?*—is a question anyone thinking about collaboration has to answer. Previously we said that in diplomacy each party needs the faith required to negotiate the issues at hand. As each party lives up to its commitments, trust is established and more complex agreements, requiring greater sharing of information, can be negotiated. It's the same in business. Listen to how Dr. Hal Varian, dean of Information Management and Systems at the University of California, Berkeley, and columnist for the *New York Times,* described how trust is built at a panel discussion on collaborative business hosted by enterprise software vendor J. D. Edwards & Company in October 2001:

> In part, you've got to have incentives set up in a way that there is something for everybody in the transaction. A lot of the trust comes out of the repeated nature of the interactions, or the contractual interaction, or the system you set up for compensation, or revenue sharing. Those are the behind-the-scenes components that really cause the trust to be created and work successfully.

Trust is not a simple concept because it encompasses ethics, emotions, values, and attitudes. As described by Kasper-Fuehrer and Ashkanasy in the May 2001 issue of the *Journal of Management,* trust results from experiencing fair behavior by the other party together with acceptance of the other party's rights and interests. An additional factor implicit in the definition of trust is the role of ethical behavior. Any change in a person's value system causes a change in behavior and thus influences trust. Trust also indicates a joint undertaking with a level of understanding of shared business practices between the parties. Finally, trust implies that the participants contribute to, and gain from, the final outcome; and this awareness of common interest and mutual benefit results in a foundation of goodwill.

> ■ **Trust results from experiencing fair** behavior by the other party and acceptance of the other party's rights and interests.

The creation of shared goals and strategy, especially in the initial stage of a relationship, facilitates collaboration on the level of the individual and on the level of the community as a whole. As such, a common business understanding provides an essential condition for the development of trust within the relationship. This understanding fosters mutual goal setting, a willingness to share information, and the creation of interpersonal trust. Communicating the importance of trustworthiness and the qualities it takes to create it throughout the Collaborative Community underlies trust building. As Kasper-Fuehrer and Ashkanasy stress, the communication of trustworthiness is an interactive and iterative process that affects, monitors, and guides people's actions and attitudes in their interactions with one another and ultimately determines the level of trust that exists between them.

You can't rush trust or simply assume that it's there. It either exists or it doesn't. And it must be reciprocal. Remember that in a collaborative relationship strategic value flows in both directions, and as such each party needs to trust the other party or otherwise the information required for the collaboration won't be shared.

LEVELS OF COLLABORATION

To get a better understanding of the importance of trust in building successful collaborative relationships, look at the Levels of Collaboration diagram in Figure 8.1. The horizontal axis repre-

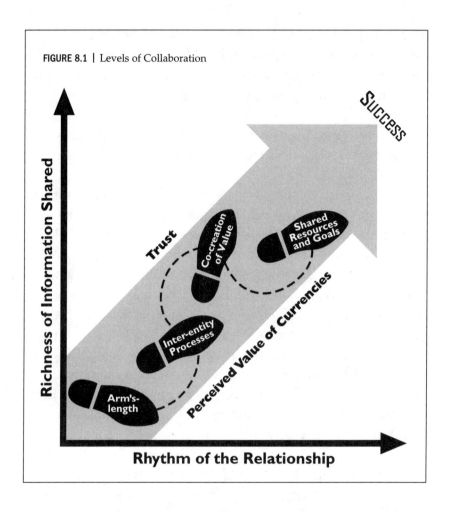

FIGURE 8.1 | Levels of Collaboration

sents the "Rhythm of the Relationship," which you recall from Chapter 5 reflects the intensity of the interactions between you and the other party. However, instead of just using the two classifications of intensity (non-intensive versus intensive), this time we've represented it as a continuum on which intensity increases.

The vertical axis represents the "Richness of Information Shared," where richness reflects a number of factors, including the quality, depth, relevancy, completeness, and timeliness of the information. For example, aggregated quarterly sales are less rich than individual customer sales when analyzing customer buying patterns.

Now let's turn our attention to the four footsteps and the underlying arrow. The footsteps represent the nature and types of activities that take place in a relationship over time. The arrow reflects both the level of "Trust" in the relationship and your ability to gain access to the "Perceived Value of Currencies" the other party can deliver. As such, trust needs to be viewed as both a prerequisite for, and a by-product of, the activities carried out and therefore directly has an impact on your ability to gain access to the inherent value in the currencies you want. In other words, the more valuable you perceive the currencies to be, the greater the richness of information you'll share and the more resources you'll commit to get those currencies.

> ■ **Trust is a prerequisite for,** and a by-product of, the activities carried out and thus directly has an impact on your ability to gain access to the currencies you want.

Essentially, what the diagram reflects is that as the level of collaboration increases, more resources and richer information are required to realize increasing benefit from the collaboration. And as the diagram demonstrates, the ability to achieve success in the era of collaborative business is dependent on building trusting and mutually beneficial collaborative relationships.

> ■ **More resources and richer information** are required to realize the increasing benefit from collaboration.

At this point, it's helpful to recall that collaboration takes place through the human relationships that carry out the collaboration as well as on the technical process–level that deals with the flow of information and activities supporting those human relationships. In this book we have addressed the human level of this interaction in our construction of the Relationship Scorecard, which establishes and prioritizes collaborative links between companies and people. In addition, we've discussed how, on the human level, the collaboration of two or more companies in conjunction with their customers requires more than establishing and prioritizing strategic links and automating information and workflows. It also requires changes in cultures and individual attitudes, and in company structures, policies, and incentive compensation systems.

According to Dr. Travis White, vice president of strategic planning for J. D. Edwards & Company, "Collaboration is right at the leading edge of a new way of doing business. There's a massive need for education, there's a need for leadership, a need for companies to stand up and build the relationships that will create their vision for the future." As we saw in Chapter 4, companies like "Company A" that are mired in legacy thinking have significant challenges in iterating their business models from the silo-creating, product-centric structures of old.

Fortunately, more and more companies, such as Milacron, Manco, Circles, and J. D. Edwards, are leading the way. Still, many companies lack belief in the value of the cultural shift required for information sharing and openness. Consequently, unless and until required by a major customer to collaborate, many companies refuse to take the step. Others, who begin down the road, don't recognize the necessity of adopting the customer's perspective and the mindset that everyone is a customer. As such, they leave in place policies and incentive systems that undermine their collaborative initiatives.

And as we have been emphasizing in this section, all of these changes on the human level of collaboration must be based on trust. Any kind of a working relationship requires trust. No matter how small the task, if two or more people are working together, each individual must trust the others' abilities and word. As Figure 8.1 shows, the level of collaboration is dependent on the level of trust, and if any company or individual is to start down the road of collaboration, then structures, cultures, attitudes, policies, and incentive compensation systems must all follow in the same direction. Otherwise, trust will not have fertile ground in which to grow. It does no good to encourage someone to collaborate if his or her pay is based on a competitive mindset.

COLLABORATIVE ACTIVITIES

Now that we've discussed the mental shifts in attitude needed for collaboration, let's look at the nature and type of activities that must be undertaken in a relationship. The four footsteps shown in Figure 8.1 represent four levels of activity. Based on our discussions in Chapter 5, the first level is designated as arm's-length.

Arm's-Length

In this type of relationship the activities are those required to facilitate a transaction between the parties. The exchange of value is non-core, as we saw in the Chapter 7 example of the CPA and his non-core, but very important, relationships with Sharon and Stephen. In many arm's-length relationships, pieces of the transaction happen electronically to reduce redundancies and increase the automation of back-office tasks. So the basic level of collaboration in many instances is automated data exchange between and among individuals and/or organizations. Common transactions like bids, purchase orders, receipts, invoices, and payments are automatically transmitted and updated. Assume, for example, a customer places an order through a Web site or via e-mail that then electronically triggers the mechanisms that prompt the supplier to service and fulfill the customer's order, whether or not with human intervention. The rhythm of such a transactional relationship is non-intensive, generally requiring few resources and only the minimum information necessary to affect that particular transaction.

The transactional experience gained allows both parties to demonstrate that they can and do adhere to the terms of the transaction, growing the trust the relationship needs if it is to develop further. But then again, it may not. The parties may only need the trust required to maintain an arm's-length relationship. Every business must have many non-core transactional relationships if it is to have the resources required to benefit from relationships that should be collaborative.

Regardless of the category within which a relationship could or should fall, in the development and maintenance of any relationship, apply the iterative business-building process first described in Chapter 2 to the process of building trust. If you remember, the process consists of four steps: assumption, preparation/testing, learning, refining new and, it's hoped, more accurate assumptions. Therefore, when applied to trust, the iterative process is an assumption of trust; preparing and testing to see if each party fulfills its obligations; learning where the problems and the successes are; refining the process to correct the problems and build on the successes; and then assuming a new level of trust.

Example of iterating an arm's-length relationship to the next level. In Chapter 5 we briefly mentioned an agricultural business we'll call the farm that was working to iterate its non-core, resource sink relationship with a not-for-profit organization into a collaborative relationship.

First, let's revisit why we considered the relationship to be a resource sink. The company that owns and operates the business has had this relationship for a number of years and felt it was strong and intensive. The two organizations had worked together on a number of initiatives, but these were really arm's-length transactions—the type of relationships both engaged in with parties where there was no commonality of interest.

Yet there were shared goals. Both organizations are committed to promoting conservation of farmland, which is why the farm has promoted and contributed to the not-for-profit's endeavors. But except for the transactional elements, the relationship was essentially one way—the farm holding annual festivals and contributing the net income from those events to the not-for-profit.

Again, there are very specific and good reasons why these contributions would continue, but we raised the question, "Could this relationship become more collaborative and benefit *both* businesses?"

In analyzing its relationship using the four questions and Relationship Scorecard, the farm discovered that even though the relationship was currently providing no real currencies of value, the not-for profit *could* offer the farm valuable currencies. In addition, the relationship already was intensive, and, most important, there were more currencies of value the farm could offer the not-for-profit. Thus, the relationship falls more precisely into the category of a Scenario B—Critical Collaborative Opportunity. The farm believes the relationship potentially represents high-value access to customers and medium-value actual validation relating to the farm's most important goal of customer acquisition. Also, the not-for-profit provides high-value intellectual property and competencies in helping the farm preserve its land for agricultural purposes and promote this cause throughout the not-for-profit's customer base.

The owners of the farm have therefore approached the not-for-profit to see if the value proposition between them could iterate and the activities between them become more collaborative. We prepared a list of the currencies the farm could offer to the not-for-profit, the most important including continued and, we hoped, increasing cash contributions, access to more than 30,000 people who visit the farm each year as potential members for the not-for-profit organization, and validation of the not-for-profit's expertise in land conservation.

Not surprisingly and despite never having entered into anything other than a transactional, arm's-length relationship with a commercial enterprise, the not-for-profit saw great value in the currencies the farm had to offer; and because of the trust built through the history of the relationship, the not-for-profit has agreed to iterate the relationship. In the first phase it will establish a simple inter-entity customer acquisition process, thus moving to the next level of collaboration and committing more resources and sharing richer information than ever before. Let's take a closer look at what we mean by inter-entity processes, the next footstep in Figure 8.1.

Inter-entity Processes

Because most people understand that working closely with other parties reduces costs and improves response times, success at the arm's-length level of activities very likely will spur collaboration at the next level, which we call inter-entity processes. Speaking to this point, Travis White of J. D. Edwards notes:

> I think one of the driving factors for this whole area of collaboration is cost reduction. Many companies I've talked with and many of our own customers have said, "The reason I want to do this is so I can see a way to reduce my costs of operation." And procurement is a natural choice for that. These types of things, such as e-procurement, are among the first levels of collaboration. I think it goes far beyond that but the first step, cost reduction, is internally driven and motivated by managers who are looking for operational efficiencies. I think over time we will see more of the win-win situations where we are developing true interchange of process and helping each other do a better job providing services to our customers.

Thus, as the relationship builds and the benefits of increased collaboration become more apparent, the parties look for ways of allowing business processes to operate on an interentity basis. This step means they facilitate the cross-organizational structuring of one or more of their three core business processes.

As a result, the parties start to share much richer information, including customer orders, inventory, fulfillment data, and so forth. For example, health-care products distributor Owens & Minor has integrated its online order fulfillment system with supplier Kimberly-Clark's product catalog system. So when Owens & Minor customers take an in-depth look at product and availability information about a Kimberly-Clark product, they are unknowingly looking at Kimberly-Clark's product catalog and ancillary resources. Such arrangements are becoming increasingly common. When all end consumers have access to a single catalog, it eliminates duplicating the catalog in different forms, significantly reducing costs to distribution partners, simplifying the update of information, and perhaps, most important, connecting Kimberly-Clark (the manufacturer) to its end consumer.

As Travis White points out, the development of many inter-entity processes is driven by the desire for cost savings in procurement. Our farm and not-for-profit, on the other hand, are sharing a customer acquisition process. The belief is that the two organizations' respective customers share mutual interests and thus represent good prospects for each other. Members of the not-for-profit will be given an incentive to visit and patronize the farm. And visitors to the farm will be given an incentive to become members of the not-for-profit. Information will need to be shared regarding who the joint customers/members are as well as the amount of their purchases so the program can be measured and managed.

Another example of inter-entity processes occurs when the management of a retailer's inventory is taken over by a supplier. In this instance, the retailer provides the supplier with all the information needed to place the orders and deliver the inventory on time. Jason Wong of Asia Foods <www.asiafoods.com> has just such a relationship with a chain of book and video stores owned by an important Chinese-language publisher. As Jason tells it, the process began when he realized that the stores didn't have a snack rack at the checkout counter, and he suggested that he supply the stores with Asian snack food. He started stocking a single store in Brooklyn, New York, and, as sales were strong, expanded across the chain. Before long, responsibility for deciding what to keep in the racks and how often to restock them was handed over to Jason. He receives daily sales data on a store-by-store basis to guide his decisions.

Integral to the inter-entity flow of information is the necessity for a transparent information structure for the shared business process. As Travis White notes, customers are asking J. D. Edwards to change the way it configures its software:

> The traditional way to configure the software was by module, or by functions, or by departments. We had financial software, manufacturing software, purchasing software, and so forth. Now customers are saying they want to buy a process as opposed to buying a function, and a popular process is [the customer-centric process] "order to cash," which is everything needed to quote a price, take an order, build a product, buy the inventory, ship, and so forth; and customers want to buy that *process* rather than a discrete set of financial software. So that process might include financial software, salesforce automation software, customer management, price management software—and that's now the way we are configuring it. The next step then is for our process to interact with the customer's process so that the order and the purchasing flow together naturally and in an automated fashion.

In many instances, collaborative initiatives encounter their first problems when the information system architecture in one company is incompatible with its partner's architecture. And as the number of entities adopting these processes increases, the problems compound. Actually, the problem of system incompatibility also happens in large, multidivisional businesses because in many instances each division makes an independent decision about what system architecture is best for its needs irrespective of what other divisions are doing.

Collaborative business models, however, require the freedom to allow disparate business systems to share information and processes. Consequently, you need to start with an architecture that enables flexibility, allowing you to quickly change the way you do business without reprogramming your information technology system. Next, you have to integrate the work and information flows of your core business processes along with the measurement framework you're using to track progress toward your goals. Finally, you need to link with your business partners and customers to optimize the processes that extend beyond your business entity.

■ **Collaborative business models require the** freedom to allow disparate business systems to share information and processes.

Collaborating through creating inter-entity processes with business partners can also run into problems in determining what information to share and in what form. Part of this fear is rooted in unwillingness to trust a business partner with valuable and, in many instances, competitive information. In addition, there is the fear that the information you receive from your partner is not reliable, but remember that this fear leads to a win-lose relationship. One or both parties conclude, "I want more information than I am willing to give," which is not a viable relationship and is why many nascent collaborations fail. The parties in viable and growing collaborations must form a comfortable trust level where they can provide access to their valued currencies and thereby gain access to the other parties' valued currencies. Thus, as we've stated, you need to balance your fear of sharing proprietary information against gaining access to the currencies required to achieve your strategic goals. We believe what allows that balance to tip toward transparency is trust built on shared experiences.

Co-creation of Value

If the parties in the relationship decide a sufficient level of trust has been established to allow them to iterate their relationship to the next level, the parties can share work and co-development activities on a real-time basis. Collaboration tools such as video conferencing, e-rooms, and virtual shared workspaces permit this sharing, thus eliminating distance. In the wake of the September 2001 terrorist attacks, these tools are enjoying greater adoption and use, but they are only effective when sufficient trust is already established.

In addition, at this level the parties can bring customers into the product and service innovation process and, along with other business partners, work on the co-creation of the market basket of goods and services needed to satisfy these customers. This is particularly important when product design and manufacture has been outsourced. According to Barry Wilderman, senior vice president of Application Strategies for META Group: "A major piece of collaboration relates to new product introduction, [as represented by] the collaboration among Nokia and its 70 suppliers to get the next generation of phones made. I think that will accelerate more, and a lot more work will be done remotely in terms of collaborating among different companies."

If the level of trust continues to develop, greater value is gained through sharing such information as real-time product design, production schedules, inventory levels, and order status. The parties can also work together to make a product, ship it, account for it, and service customers. At this level, the parties don't just share data and information; they co-manage activities through automated core business processes that span their companies. It is also likely that their inter-company information system is structured such that access to information is dependent on the need to know. In other words, people will see different information depending on whether they are customers or business partners. Clearly, the ability to limit each party's information access is critical given the inherent security concerns and the proprietary nature of each party's information.

How two entrepreneurial businesses are co-creating value. When Jon Aram of Responsible World (a business that helps companies pursue innovative programs in community relations and social responsibility) met Kevin McCall of Paradigm Properties (a developer and manager of commercial real estate), they both recognized that they valued community involvement as an integral part of doing business. Jon was looking for a distribution partner to help him reach customers and develop his understanding of the customer need for community relations programs his business intends to solve. Kevin was looking to add product development and expertise about community relations into his company's mix of competencies. Soon Jon was collaborating with Kevin to jointly develop community relations products and services for the smaller to midsized businesses that are Kevin's tenants (customers). So just as in the Dave and Max story, Jon receives access to potential customers and Kevin gets a new product and thus a revenue stream his competitors don't have.

Shared Resources and Goals

The highest level of collaborative activity requires sharing resources and goals. At this level of collaboration, you realize the greatest value potential because efficiencies and innovations flow through multiple businesses. You're no longer going it alone. You think of your customers and business partners as part of your organization, and as each entity works to satisfy its respective needs and goals, it contributes to the others' achieving their needs and goals. It is at this level of collaboration that you have built your Collaborative Community. Think back to the discussion about Circles, the Boston-based choreographer discussed in Chapter 3. It works jointly with its distribution partners to develop "lifetime value and loyalty" programs for its partners' customers and/or employees. And it works jointly with its suppliers, bringing them customers to fulfill the programs' services. According to CEO Janet Kraus, "Listening to the needs, capturing the data, and driving value to all of the constituents is the power of the choreographer." Let's look at how Circles is using this power to expand its already highly collaborative relationships.

In talking with its distribution partners (Circles' primary customers), Circles discovered that these partners wanted access to the data Circles was assembling in the process of fulfilling its services. Think about it. When consumers (whom Circles calls members) interact with a Circles personal assistant (concierge) or access Circles' member Web site, Circles collects tremendous amounts of unique data about that member, its needs, and the solutions to those needs. Circles has always known there is great value in the data but hadn't yet turned it into a revenue stream. Now, as Janet says, "We're sitting next to the customer, as its partner in really thinking about loyalty overall. We're going to the next step and helping the customer understand and interpret the information."

Janet continues: "Now you've developed a relationship with the member [through a concierge]. This is a very non-intrusive vehicle that people want to interact with, as opposed to a telemarketer or a bland piece of direct mail. The concierge asks questions, the answers to which become part of your data set around members."

As Janet sees it, this relationship and the data it brings are allowing Circles to bring greater and greater value to everyone in its Collaborative Community. Let's take a closer look at how the value proposition Circles offers to its community has grown over time:

Phase 1 Value Proposition:

- Member (Consumer): Gets something done/saves time

- Distribution partner (Customer): Brand in front of member/ positive association

- Supplier partner: Gains revenue on transaction

- Circles: Data

Phase 2 Value Proposition:

- Member: Gets something done more quickly/less effort

- Distribution partner: Brand loyalty begins to kick in, cross-sell opportunities

- Supplier partner: Begins to see a better pattern/gets a better deal cut

- Circles: More data, barrier to exit [as relationship builds]

Phase 3 Value Proposition:

- Member: Relevance/discounted access/exclusive access

- Distribution partner: True relationships with member/ more cross-sell/strong barriers to exit

- Supplier partner: Predictable, forecastable revenue

- Circles: More data, barrier to exit for distribution partner

All of these are win-win relationships.

As Circles builds on its core competency, Janet is very clear that Circles will do so through establishing relationships with companies that have the necessary additional competencies, particularly in the area of data analysis. For example, she says she wants to partner with a company that has "an analytical methodology (relationship currency of intellectual property) and data-intensive people (relationship currency of competencies) who can take data and set up models to figure out what patterns are emerging." Circles essentially created the Web-based personal assistance market. As it becomes increasingly competitive on obvious attributes, it is expanding its position "to understand the larger context within which it can partner and compete for better differentiation and higher value." As Janet contends, Circles will continue to grow by "broadening our breadth of services and leveraging the power of our customers' and members' relationships."

Circles has been building a Collaborative Community since 1998, having had the entrepreneur's advantage of starting with a "clean sheet of paper." An example of how established companies can experiment with this level of collaboration, one relationship at a time, was told by Paul McDougall in the May 7, 2001, issue of *InformationWeek:*

> It's a summer morning in Atlanta, the kind where the warm dawn invariably gives way to a hot, still afternoon. A pickup pulls into the lot of a local Home Depot store and out climbs a worker, lunchbox in hand. He enters the store and uses a keypad to log into a mobile cart that will track his hours as he helps shoppers in the store's lumberyard. It's a perfectly ordinary beginning to a perfectly ordinary day—except that this man doesn't work for Home Depot. Rather, he's an employee of Georgia-Pacific Corp.
>
> So why is he punching the clock at Home Depot? In the coming months, the lumber maker and the home-improvement retailer will test whether working together can improve customer service and sales. Under the pilot plan, Home Depot will collect data from the time cards of product representatives, marry

. . . [them] with sales and inventory information, and forward [them] electronically to Georgia-Pacific. The idea: By providing its top suppliers with more detailed information about how its people perform on the store floor, Home Depot hopes to increase its sales as well as those of its suppliers. "Hopefully, we'll both end up managing a better business together," Home Depot CIO Ron Griffin says. (Reprinted with permission of *Information Week*, CMP Media, Manhasset, NY)

One other point regarding the four levels of collaboration: As a result of preexisting conditions, such as people who already know each other or each other's reputations, or the specifics of a situation at hand, it is possible for a relationship to start at any of the four levels. But no matter at which level a relationship begins, it begins because the trust required for that level of collaboration exists. Nonetheless, the parties to the relationship must ensure that they put in place the necessary safeguards so that concerns about security of information and trust are always considered. Essentially, if you can start a collaboration at levels 2, 3, or even 4, you must ensure that all of the issues inherent at each level are dealt with, or the desired collaboration won't work.

THE RISKS OF COLLABORATION

Clearly, increasing the level of collaboration does have risks. In addition to the issue of information risk that is present at all levels of collaboration, engaging in inter-entity processes, co-creation of value, or the sharing of resources and goals introduces currency risk. And it also raises fundamental questions such as: How will the collaboration be governed and managed? Who owns any intellectual property resulting from the collaboration? Where does one company's liability end and another's begin given the shared nature of the collaborative activities? These questions and issues regarding how value and risk are created and shared among the parties to the collaboration reflect the challenges facing anyone building collaborative relationships.

As the diagram in Figure 8.1 illustrates, the benefit of collaboration—that is, goal attainment through greater and more purposeful access to, and use of, relationship currencies—is only realizable as trust increases. As we've said, trust increases most directly by doing what you say you'll do, when you say you'll do it. And along with the increase in trust required to gain access to the other party's currencies come the risks you create by granting others access to *your* currencies. Let's take a closer look at some of the risks and questions surrounding collaboration:

Information Risk

Everyone worries, to some degree, about the potential misuse and outright abuse of his or her information, whether personal or business related. However, every businessperson and every company collects information about the people and companies it does business with. Thus, *everyone* has an obligation to safeguard non-public information. Although to what degree is the subject of debate, in a collaborative environment, where the transparent flow of information is central to success, information must be safeguarded to whatever degree is required to keep it flowing. This isn't a simple task. Non-disclosure agreements are difficult to enforce, and even if they are enforceable, the damage has already been done. Copyrights and patents offer a greater degree of protection, but again only from a reactive posture. Most important, maintaining the necessary flow of information boils down to the three basic tenets of collaborative relationships: trustworthiness, purposefulness, and mutual benefit.

■ **The basic tenets of collaborative** relationships are trustworthiness, purposefulness, and mutual benefit.

Transparency of information only exists if the party making the information available believes it is secure. Consequently, the needs of the information provider must be met or the provider will stop making the information available. For example, a company will not share its sales forecast with a supplier regardless of the benefit if it believes the supplier would misuse that information. Thus, every business's system of internal controls should include policies, procedures, and monitoring adequate to safeguard information.

A company's information security infrastructure should include firewalls, passwords, restricted access, and other technical and physical protections. In addition, the business entity collecting information has the responsibility to be up front and to clearly, consistently, and continuously explain what information it collects and tracks and how it intends to use that information.

Currency Risk

Systematically trading in relationship currencies carries the risk of over-promising and then underdelivering in that you can't offer the same currency to too many people. For example, our CPA in Chapter 7 can't offer every banker in town access to his clients; his clients would resent a string of bankers calling, and the bankers would find that the CPA's referrals had little value. That would make it difficult for the CPA to continue to offer his now devalued currency of access to customers.

An additional risk is not recognizing soon enough that you have incorrectly identified the currencies needed to achieve your goals. For example, you may have thought you needed validation of the benefits of your product, but you subsequently realize you must improve customer service before you can obtain that validation. This realization means you must first get the currency that gives you the competencies needed to improve customer service. Such changing of priorities, which is a common occurrence, is why we have emphasized the need to quickly validate or invalidate your underlying assumptions, including your assumptions about the specific currencies needed.

Governance and Management

As we stated in Chapter 1, traditional business and industry structures are dying. The rigid corporate structures of the past don't accommodate the fluid alliances required for success in the era of collaborative business, a fact that has led to a period of experimentation with the structure and management of collaborative relationships.

Although the list is not exhaustive, we offer the following ground rules for successful collaborations:

- Collaborations must have a specific purpose and thus a specific end point.

- Decision-making authority must be entrusted to the individual responsible for the activity associated with that decision.

- Milestones and business processes must be mutually agreed to before activity commences.

- Ownership of, and the rights to use, intellectual property arising from a collaboration must be agreed to at the outset.

- Metrics and the methods of measurement should be determined before activity is under way.

- Operating responsibilities must be clear and proportionate to potential reward; incentives must thus align with responsibilities.

- All agreements should provide for easy iteration of roles, responsibilities, and rewards as each party gains knowledge about what it can give to and get from the collaboration.

Obviously, risks are inherent in developing collaborative relationships, but we believe the greater risk is not collaborating.

❚ **The greatest risk is the** risk of not collaborating.

Companies looking to adopt collaborative business practices for the first time should start with small steps to get both sides used to the relationship and pay close attention to what information is passed back and forth. Then, by following the iterative process, they should work through the levels of collaboration, carefully building the trust needed to gain access to the currencies that will bring success.

GETTING THE RIGHT INFORMATION TO THE RIGHT PERSON AT THE RIGHT TIME

Regardless of the specific level and richness of information you're sharing, *your information infrastructure must get the right information to the right person at the right time.* And while this is always the goal of any information technology architecture, the complexity of realizing this objective increases significantly as you start to collaborate with more customers and business partners. We've seen that you can have different collaborative activities occurring with different partners at the same time. Lenley Hensarling, vice president of Collaborative Technologies at J. D. Edwards, is keenly aware of this: "We, as software vendors, have to come to grips with making things flexible enough to meet the needs of all of the [collaborative] models. What we see in our customers is [that] even a single customer has to play in multiple models."

Because we're talking about the requirement to get information to the right person at the right time, it is instructive to understand just how much our access to information and the speed with which information moves have changed. When the United States won the American Revolution in 1781, it took King George six weeks to get the news. Some 84 years later, when President Abraham Lincoln was assassinated in April 1865, it took the citizens of England two weeks to learn of his death. When the Japanese attacked Pearl Harbor in December 1941, every country in the world knew about it within 24 hours. Yet by September 11, 2001, when the second plane hit the second World Trade Center tower, it was watched live by people in every country on the planet.

Clearly, access to real-time information is now an accepted part of our lives. Nevertheless, you must make certain that your company's information infrastructure has certain general characteristics to support the goals of collaboration. These ten characteristics are:

1. The information infrastructure must allow you to effectively allocate your resources to those relationships (both internal and external to the company) that are of the greatest strategic value. As such, the information infrastructure has to provide you with the information required to value, measure, and manage your relationships.

2. The information infrastructure of all companies in your community must facilitate collaboration with all customers and business partners in your community. Customers and business partners increasingly require transparent access into the ordering, product development, and fulfillment processes. Business partners need knowledge of consumers' buying patterns to better manage their own resources.

3. The information infrastructure needs to support rapid and knowledgeable decision making from the customers' point of view as well as encourage and enable

iteration of your core business processes, collaborative activities, and the information architecture itself.

4. Of critical importance is the ability to understand the flow of one's business on a real-time basis so that you can make the necessary changes on a real-time basis. Critical metrics data must also be available in real time and accessible from anywhere. So too must technical support.

5. The information infrastructure must present a personal view of the relevant relationships to every individual concerned, whether a business partner or a customer, as all have specific sets of information required to carry out their activities. The information infrastructure must provide each person with precise information exactly when needed.

6. The information infrastructure must automate the information flow for all core business processes and establish accountability at the task level. A company's information infrastructure must not only gather information but must aid in the use of that information by driving the business processes it affects across your business and across all partners.

7. Knowledge of customers and business partners must be shared. Even though not all users will have access to all the data and information, everyone must have access to what he or she needs. Just as the business infrastructure opens itself to customers and business partners, so too must the information infrastructure. It shouldn't matter where information resides within the community. Any member who needs it should have access to it.

8. The information infrastructure must facilitate the community's strict adherence to established privacy poli-

cies and provide for a sufficient level of information security for all. In addition, users must have the ability to review the accuracy of their personal information and effect any required changes.

9. The information infrastructure must be operational without intense and time-consuming up-front definition. It needs to be defined by the needs of the business, not the preset parameters of an application designed without knowledge of the business.

10. And perhaps most important, the information infrastructure must assist you in "seeing" the patterns in the information. How many data points do you need before you see a pattern? With better intuition you need fewer. If your intuition isn't so well developed, you need more data. The information infrastructure has to support your ability to see the important patterns. However, how completely they need to be drawn before they are recognized will forever be based on the skill and experience of the individual involved.

Now that we've looked at the different levels of collaboration and the types of activities through which you build the trust and develop the relationships necessary to gain valued currencies, it's time to focus on how to use those currencies to achieve your goals.

WHAT HAVE WE LEARNED?

1 ▌ Just because someone has currencies that could benefit you, that person is not going to offer them unless the required trust exists and you identify currencies you have that he or she wants.

2 ∎ Trust results from experiencing fair behavior by the other party together with accepting the other party's rights and interests.

3 ∎ Trust needs to be viewed as both a prerequisite for, and a by-product of, the activities carried out and therefore directly impacts your ability to gain access to the inherent value in the currencies you want.

4 ∎ The richness of the information shared reflects a number of factors, including the quality, depth, relevancy, completeness, and timeliness of the information.

5 ∎ As the level of collaboration increases, more resources and richer information are required to realize the increasing benefit from the collaboration.

6 ∎ The level of collaboration is dependent on the level of trust, and if any company or individual is to start down the road of collaboration, then structures, cultures, attitudes, policies, and incentive compensation systems must all follow in the same direction.

7 ∎ When applied to trust, the iterative process here is an assumption of trust; preparing and testing to see if each party fulfills its obligations; learning where the problems and the successes are; refining the process to correct the problems and build on the successes; and then assuming a new level of trust.

8 ∎ There are four levels of collaborative activities: (1) arm's-length; (2) inter-entity processes; (3) co-creation of value; and (4) shared resources and goals.

9 ∎ The basic level of collaboration in many instances is automated data exchange among individuals and/or organizations.

10 ∎ Inter-entity processes are the cross-organizational structuring of one or more of the three core business processes.

11 ■ At the co-creation of value level, major activities involve using technology to work collaboratively, notably in the area of new product development and introduction.

12 ■ The highest level of collaborative activity requires sharing resources and goals. At this level of collaboration, you realize the greatest value potential because efficiencies and innovations flow through multiple businesses. It is at this level of collaboration that you have built your Collaborative Community.

13 ■ Collaborative business models require the freedom to share information and processes among disparate business systems.

14 ■ In addition to the issue of information risk that is present at all levels of collaboration, engaging in inter-entity processes, co-creating value, or sharing resources and goals introduces currency risk.

15 ■ Maintaining the necessary flow of information boils down to the three basic tenets of collaborative relationships: trustworthiness, purposefulness, and mutual benefit.

16 ■ Obviously, risks are inherent in developing collaborative relationships, but the greater risk is not collaborating.

17 ■ As you start to collaborate with more customers and business partners, the complexity of getting the right information to the right person at the right time increases significantly.

CHAPTER 9

Using Relationship Currencies to Achieve Your Goals

I n the last chapter, we took a detailed look at how you gain access to cash and non-cash currencies as you iterate a relationship though the four activity levels of collaboration (Figure 8.1). As you gain access to those non-cash relationship currencies, you need to think about how you can use them to help you achieve your goals.

CURRENCY USE GUIDELINES

To understand how to use currencies to achieve your goals, we'll review and add to the guidelines first described in Chapter 4:

- You don't have to convert all non-cash relationship currencies into cash because in many instances non-cash currencies have greater value than cash.

▮ In many instances non-cash relationship currencies have greater value than cash.

- You have to make assumptions about the specific currencies you'll need to achieve your goals.

- A currency has value only if you have it when needed.

- You must determine the time value of the currencies received in the sense of whether they will appreciate or depreciate over time.

- The value of a relationship currency is determined only by the recipient of that currency.

- A relationship currency may have to be combined with other cash and non-cash currencies for it to be of value to the recipient.

- You can use the relationship currencies you have (whether yours to begin with or received from someone else) in value propositions you establish with other parties.

▮ You can use the currencies received from someone else in value propositions you establish with other parties.

- You can "bank" non-cash relationship currencies as you are now able to measure and account for them.

- You may have to convert one relationship currency into another before you can use it. These conversions may be carried out with one or more people.

- You have to be careful to not overcommit the currencies you are providing to others.

Given these guidelines, let's look more closely at how you use currencies to achieve your goals.

RELATIONSHIP LINKAGE

As an example of how this process works, we'll examine one of our own experiences mentioned in the preface. In January 2001, we were asked to deliver a keynote speech at the Delphi Group's Collaborative Commerce Summit held in June 2001. To assist us in evaluating that speaking opportunity, we prepared a Relationship Scorecard for the Delphi Group. As you can see in Figure 9.1, we believed we could potentially receive, in addition to any cash compensation, four non-cash currencies: (1) actual validation as experts in collaborative business (as we would be making a keynote speech); (2) access to potential customers (the hundreds of attendees at the Summit); (3) information about technology (collaborative commerce software solutions from attendees and exhibitors); and (4) access to competencies (the talented people we would meet). As shown in the Relationship Scorecard we prepared (Figure 9.2), the four goals we focused on achieving by December 31, 2001, were related to our cash flow requirements and our three core business processes: (1) cus-

FIGURE 9.1 | Anticipated Currencies from Collaborative Commerce Summit

Currencies / Levels	Information About	Access To	Actual Currency
Cash			✓
Customers		✓	
Products and Services			
Competencies		✓	
Validation			✓
Technology	✓		
Intellectual Property			

FIGURE 9.2 | Delphi Group Relationship Scorecard

Name: Tom at Delphi Group Future Date : 1/15/01				
Goal Weighting (100%)	40%	20%	20%	20%
Currencies Goals	CA&R	P&SI	CF&S	CASH
Cash				3
Customers	2			
Products and Services				
Competencies			3	
Validation	5			
Technology		2		
Intellectual Property				
Other				
Weighted Totals	2.8	0.4	0.6	0.6
Relationship Value (RV)	4.4			

Currency Level			
Utility		Information About	Access To	Actual Currency
	Low	1	2	3
	Medium	2	3	4
	High	3	4	5

tomer acquisition and retention (CA&R); (2) product and service innovation (P&SI); and (3) customer fulfillment and service (CF&S). We calculated Delphi's Future Relationship Value (FRV) to be 4.4. That is, based on our assumptions, we believed that the value we would receive toward helping us achieve our goals for 2001 was 4.4. We then prioritized that value relative to the FRVs we had calculated for other opportunities and made the decision to accept the invitation to speak at the summit.

This decision led to an increase in the intensity of our relationship with Delphi as a result of our allocating more resources to it. The reason we needed to allocate more resources was due to the specific activities we had to carry out in preparing for our summit presentation. These activities included several face-to-face meetings, e-mail exchanges, and numerous telephone conversations during the months leading up to the summit. In addition, we conducted a focused research study on choreographers to augment the information we wanted to present, and we worked with a graphic designer on the visuals we'd use in our presentation. As the time of the summit approached, we composed and sent a number of e-mail announcements publicizing our participation.

Because we are focusing on how to use currencies to achieve goals, let's now examine how we derived value from the currencies we received from Delphi. In Figure 9.3, we've laid out the 12-month timeline for 2001 and have identified both the relationships developed as a result of our participation at the summit and the currencies we believed we would receive from those relationships. The currencies shown in Figure 9.3 are what we thought we'd gain from those relationships (their future value) as identified at the time we first met a particular person. This analysis includes only the new relationships that sprang directly from our presentation and attendance at the summit. The currencies we received from Delphi and from the other relationships were not all made available to us in our first interactions. As noted in Chapter 8, you gain access to currencies as relationships iterate through the different activity levels

FIGURE 9.3 | Relationship Linkage Diagram, Delphi Group

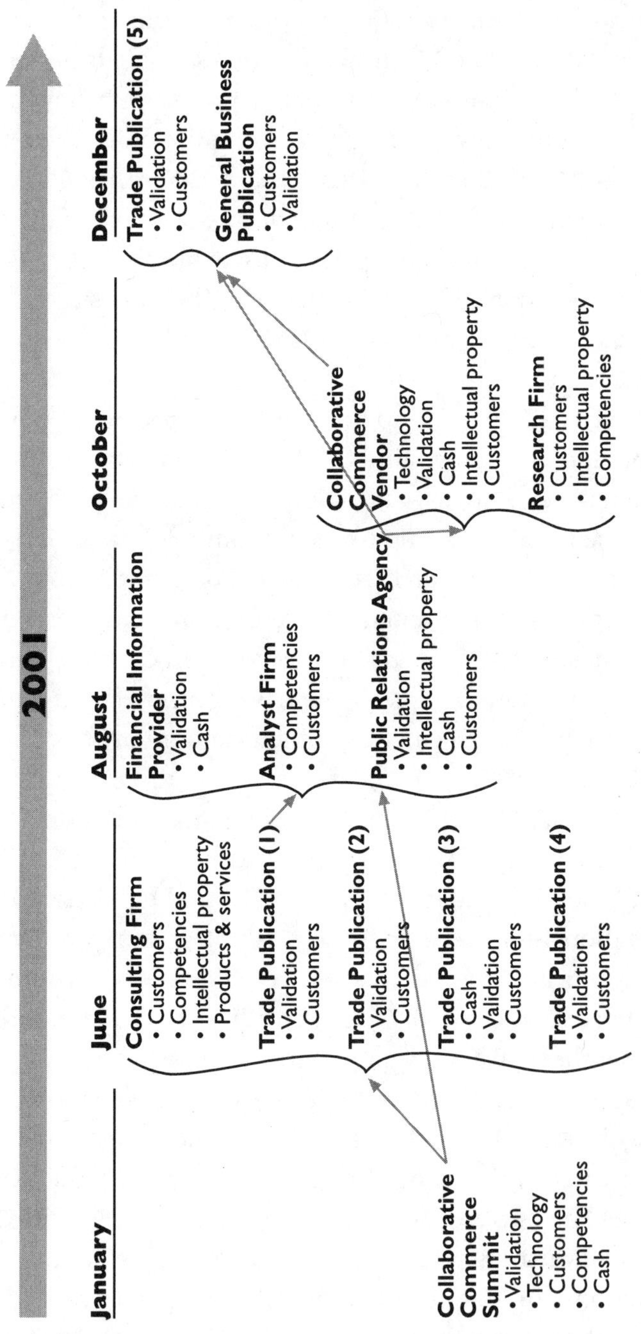

of collaboration. Understanding this, we engaged in a number of interactions with each of the relationships that came out of our presentation and attendance at the summit. Some eventually resulted in helping us achieve our goals. Some did not. (Please note: To protect the privacy of our business associates, we are using generic business categories rather than naming specific companies and individuals.)

Now let's take a closer look at some of the relationships shown in Figure 9.3.

BUILDING NEW RELATIONSHIPS

The first new relationship identified in Figure 9.3 was with a managing principal of a West Coast consulting company. As can be seen, it was our belief at the time that this relationship could provide the following currencies: (1) access to the company's intellectual property; (2) actual competencies of the managing principal and other staff; (3) access to the company's base of consulting clients; and (4) the joint development of a new product that would benefit our respective customer bases. It was this fourth currency that we saw as the primary value accruing from the relationship.

Directly below the consulting company, we listed two trade publications that wrote about the ideas we presented and/or based articles on an interview with us. Not only has one of these publications subsequently asked us to write for their publication, but representatives of two other trade publications that heard us speak have also asked us to write for their online and offline magazines and are listed as Trade Publications (3) and (4). Each of these four trade publications has provided us with some combination of the following currencies: (1) cash, (2) validation, and (3) customers (their readers interested in learning about collaboration).

Let's shift focus now to our relationship with the public relations (PR) agency. Approximately two months after the summit, we received a telephone call from John, a vice president of one of the largest public relations companies in the world. John said that he had read about us in Trade Publication (1), and as shown in Figure 9.3, he had also perused the program schedule for the summit on the Delphi Group Web site and knew we had given a keynote speech on collaborative business. He said he was calling on behalf of a client, a major collaborative commerce software vendor. John said he was assembling a "panel of experts" on collaborative business and asked if we would participate on the panel. After the telephone conversation, we prepared a Relationship Scorecard for John, having first identified the currencies we thought we'd gain access to as a result of our participation: (1) validation (recognition as an expert on collaborative business); (2) intellectual property (the knowledge coming out of the panel); (3) cash (for participation on the panel); and (4) access to customers (the software company and the PR agency's other clients).

In Figure 9.4, we calculated a Future Relationship Value of 5.2 for John at the agency, which was higher than the 4.4 value we had calculated for Delphi in January. This means that despite the fact that it was already mid-August, we believed that the value of the currencies we'd receive from the PR agency was greater than Delphi's, even though we were almost two-thirds through the year (thus leaving little time to make use of the currencies to realize our 2001 goals). After completing the scorecard, we decided to participate, taking into consideration not only what we'd gain from our participation but also the impact on our resources, as we knew preparing for the panel would require a number of resource-consuming activities. Remember, there is always a give and get to a collaborative relationship.

In early October 2001, we participated in the panel discussion. For us, it was a very interesting experience. Not only did we meet and interact with several nationally known media personalities and business experts, but we also began a relationship with the software company on whose behalf the event was orga-

FIGURE 9.4 | PR Agency Relationship Scorecard, August 2001

Name: **John at PR Agency Future** Date : **8/27/01**				
Goal Weighting (100%)	40%	20%	20%	20%
Currencies Goals	CA&R	P&SI	CF&S	CASH
Cash				3
Customers	5			
Products and Services				
Competencies				
Validation	5			
Technology				
Intellectual Property		3		
Other				
Weighted Totals	4.0	0.6		0.6
Relationship Value (RV)	5.2			

		Currency Level		
		Information About	Access To	Actual Currency
Utility	Low	1	2	3
	Medium	2	3	4
	High	3	4	5

nized. In addition, as shown in Figure 9.3, one of the other panelists, a senior vice president at a major research firm, has asked us to present our work on measuring the value of relationships to a group of his firm's analysts.

Again referring to Figure 9.3, you can see that we are building a relationship with the collaborative commerce vendor as a result of our participation on the panel. As with the other relationships shown, we've identified the currencies we believe we'll access as we build our relationship over time.

Although we haven't described every relationship in detail, let's move on and explore how we realized value from the currencies we accessed in all of these relationships.

VALUE REALIZED

As we've discussed throughout this book, the primary benefit of purposeful collaboration is to allocate your resources to those relationships that provide the currencies you need for achieving your goals. Consequently, you must continuously evaluate whether the currencies you have gained and used are in fact enabling you to achieve what you want to accomplish. To do this, you should compare the planned milestone against the actual level achieved, as shown in Figure 9.5. Having a planned milestone requires that you also identify how a goal is to be measured (the M in S-M-A-R-T) when you set your goals. For example, if your goal is to increase sales by 50 percent, then the metric would be the actual increase in sales over the prior period.

However, if you are only monitoring the percentage increase in sales, you'll not be successful, as that metric represents the results at the end of the sales process. What we believe is more critical is to identify a simple predictive metric early in the sales process that is as near to real-time data as possible. For example, perhaps it's the number of customer inquiries per day, or the number of product demos conducted each week, or the number of people who enter your store each hour. Bear in mind the best metric may not be directly connected to the sales process. For example, one of the best metrics for gauging sales in a fast-food restaurant is the average length of time it takes to

FIGURE 9.5 | Evaluate Performance

Goal Number	Planned Level	Actual Level	Achieved Goal Yes/No
1			
2			
3			
4			

serve a customer. A manager doesn't have to wait to see the day's sales to take action. As soon as he observes it is taking longer to serve a customer than desired, he can quickly reshuffle personnel to correct the situation.

■ **Identify a simple metric that** is as near to real-time data as possible.

Let's take a closer look at this evaluation process. Recall that in Figure 7.3 (Chapter 7), the example we presented identified as Goal 1 signing up five business clients who require business planning, audit, and tax services. However, the reality is you should not wait until the end of the goal achievement period, which in this example is year-end 2003, to see if you signed up the desired five new clients. Your information system should provide the specific information you require so that you can assess progress toward your goals at any time. Again, the metric is not the number of clients already signed up but something occurring much earlier in the process, such as the number of meetings you have with prospects.

One of the primary benefits of using the Relationship Scorecard is that it provides you with a real-time indication of whether you are making progress toward your goals. By using it to record the currencies you are receiving on an interaction-by-interaction basis, you'll always know if you are gaining access to the desired currencies when you need them. If you aren't getting what you need when you need it, you aren't making progress. Thus, if a person's current relationship value doesn't increase after an interaction with that person, you haven't received additional currencies and thus haven't made progress toward the goals those currencies are supposed to help you achieve. By using currencies to monitor your progress on a real-time basis, you can iterate how and to whom you're allocating your resources as soon as you sense that it's necessary to make an adjustment. This rapid assessment and subsequent adjustment increase the likelihood you will accomplish your plans.

▌ **If you aren't getting the** currencies you need when you need them, you aren't making progress.

The Relationship Scorecard helps you measure and manage your relationships so that you can better reach your goals and gain success. And the table in Figure 9.5 allows you to regularly monitor your progress toward the milestone you've established for each goal. Essentially, this evaluation is best thought of as that step in the iterative process we call analysis and refinement.

You use our analytical tools and your information system to provide you with real-time data, and then based on your ability to "see the patterns" where and when necessary, you refine your actions to gain the currencies and achieve your goals.

■ **Rapid assessment and subsequent adjustment** increase the likelihood you will accomplish your planned level of achievement.

Given this understanding, let's take a look at the value we realized from our initial decision to accept Delphi's offer. (This analysis does not include our use of currencies received from these new relationships with people known prior to the summit. As such, the listing does not include *all* of the value we realized from our presentation and attendance.) As of December 31, 2001, Delphi Group and the 12 other people/companies with whom we've established relationships have provided the following value:

- Seven bylined articles published

- Three articles written about us

- Two relationships developed with people who add significant competencies to our community

- Cash compensation in excess of five times cash expended

- A bylined article placed in a major business publication by the PR agency

- An initial assignment with the software vendor

- A presentation to a major research firm

- References to us and quotes from us in numerous publications as experts in collaborative business

Clearly, the above items added significantly toward the achievement of our goals for 2001. But that's not the whole story. In addition to our relationship with the Delphi Group, we now have 12 new relationships (members) in our community and can assess the value of their currencies relative to helping us achieve our goals for 2002. So, like the Energizer Bunny, the process keeps on going and going and going.

Figure 9.6 is the scorecard for our association with the PR agency as of early January 2002 in relation to our new goal priorities for the year. As you can see, not only have we changed the weighting on each goal, but we felt that we could access additional relationship currencies from the PR agency, resulting in a new Future Relationship Value of 7.45. The reason we felt we would gain access to additional currencies was because of the value of the currencies we have already received (thus closing the Delta) as we've iterated our relationship with John through the first two levels of collaboration (shown in Figure 9.7). As we write this book, we are just starting to work together at the co-creation of value level, as we're helping John implement the Relationship Scorecard process in his dealings with his customers. We think it will be an important tool for him to demonstrate to customers the value his services bring, and it will help us create a new product.

PUTTING IT ALL TOGETHER

Thus, using relationship currencies to help you achieve goals is really a process of recognizing the value of non-cash currencies and the categories they fall into, such as access to intellectual property, information about customers, and so forth. Then, by evaluating your relationships and the currencies they bring, you put in place purposeful value propositions with specific members of your community and work diligently to use those currencies to achieve your goals. This last point may seem

FIGURE 9.6 | PR Agency Relationship Scorecard, January 2002

Name: **John at PR Agency** **Future** Date: 1/7/02				
Goal Weighting (100%)	35%	25%	25%	15%
Currencies Goals	**CA&R**	**P&SI**	**CF&S**	**CASH**
Cash				3
Customers	5	4		
Products and Services	5			
Competencies				
Validation	5			
Technology				
Intellectual Property		3		
Other				
Weighted Totals	5.25	1.75		.45
Relationship Value (RV)	7.45			

		Currency Level		
		Information About	Access To	Actual Currency
Utility	Low	1	2	3
	Medium	2	3	4
	High	3	4	5

obvious, but we don't know how many times businesspeople fail to take advantage of relationship currencies. For example, businesspeople agree to give a speech and then fail to network after the speech, have articles placed for them but aren't ready

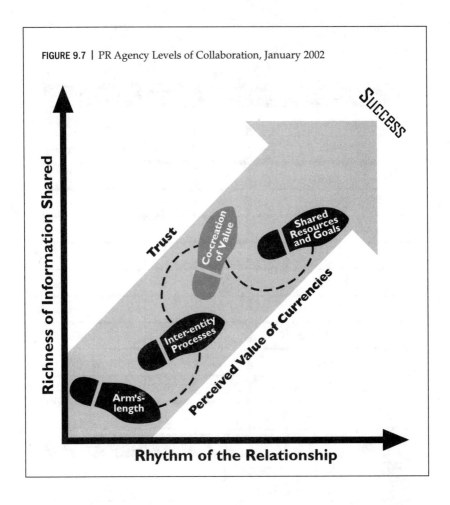

FIGURE 9.7 | PR Agency Levels of Collaboration, January 2002

Richness of Information Shared

SUCCESS

Trust

Co-creation of Value

Shared Resources and Goals

Inter-entity Processes

Arm's-length

Perceived Value of Currencies

Rhythm of the Relationship

to exploit the publicity, and/or gain access to a potential client but fail to impress the client. In short, non-cash currencies only make sense if you can take advantage of a specific currency.

An offer that allows you to network is worth nothing if you are a poor networker. Publicity is of no value if you don't take advantage of the publicity. An interview with a valuable client is a mistake unless you are prepared to impress the client. Therefore, when evaluating which non-cash currencies offer the most potential at any particular point, you must take into consideration your own and your company's strengths and weaknesses. Then, if you decide to go ahead based on receiving the relationship currencies, you must follow up that decision by working hard to transform that currency into what you need to achieve your goals.

We hope this discussion has not only provided you with a better understanding of how to use non-cash currencies but has also shown you how to utilize all your currencies when negotiating with other parties. After all, once you understand the value of relationship currencies and how to evaluate them for yourself, it's easy to see how *your* currencies might be of value to others and how best to present them.

Like many things in business, it may take some practice to use the processes and tools discussed in this chapter (and throughout the book) before they become second nature to you. However, the return on the investment will be significant. Not only will you build collaborative relationships but for the very first time you can effectively focus your resources on those relationships that provide you the greatest strategic benefit.

WHAT HAVE WE LEARNED?

1 ∎ Below are ten guidelines for using non-cash relationship currencies to achieve your goals:

- You do not have to convert all non-cash relationship currencies into cash because in many instances non-cash currencies have greater value than cash.

- You have to make assumptions about the specific currencies you'll need to achieve your goals.

- A currency has value only if you have it when needed.

- You have to determine the time value of the currencies received in the sense of whether they will appreciate or depreciate over time.

- The value of a relationship currency is determined only by the recipient of that currency.

- A relationship currency may have to be combined with other cash and non-cash currencies to be of value to the recipient.

- You can use the relationship currencies you have (whether they're yours to begin with or received from someone else) in value propositions you establish with other parties.

- You can "bank" non-cash relationship currencies, as you are now able to account for them.

- You may have to convert one relationship currency into another before you can use it. Such conversions may be carried out with one or more people.

- You have to be careful to not overcommit the currencies you are providing to others.

2 ∎ Continually evaluate whether the currencies you have gained and used are in fact enabling you to achieve what you want by comparing the planned milestone against the actual level achieved.

3 ∎ We believe it is critical to identify a simple metric early on in the process you are monitoring that is as near to real-time data as possible.

4 ∎ By using the Relationship Scorecard to record the currencies you are receiving on an interaction-by-interaction basis, you'll always know if you are gaining access to the desired currencies when you need them. If you aren't getting what you need when you need it, you aren't making progress.

5 ∎ By monitoring your progress on a real-time basis, you can iterate how you're allocating your resources as soon as you sense that it's necessary. This rapid assessment and adjustment increase the likelihood you will accomplish your planned level of achievements.

6 ▮ Using currencies to help you achieve goals is really a process of recognizing the value of non-cash currencies and the categories they fall into, such as access to intellectual property, information about customers, and so forth. Then, by evaluating relationships and the currencies they bring, you put in place purposeful value propositions with specific members of your community and work diligently to use these currencies to achieve your goals. You analyze the results, make new assumptions, and start the process again.

PART THREE

Choreographing
Your Success

CHAPTER 10

How *You* Do Business in the Era of Collaborative Business

ARE YOU READY TO COLLABORATE?

Is *your* company ready to collaborate? Are *you*? The knowledge and understanding gained by reading this book, we hope, has prepared you for our readiness check for collaborative business. Be honest with yourself as you answer these ten important questions:

	YES	NO
1. Are you ready to look at every relationship as a customer relationship?	_____	_____
2. Are you ready to allocate your resources to those relationships that provide the greatest strategic value?	_____	_____
3. Are you ready to put in place a company structure, compensation system, and culture that foster internal and external collaboration?	_____	_____

4. Are you ready to engage your customers and business partners in the design, development, and delivery of the market basket of goods and services intended to satisfy your customers?   _____ _____

5. Are you ready to measure and manage the relationships that comprise your community and underlie your day-to-day activities?   _____ _____

6. Are you ready to systematically track the individual interactions you have with your customers and business partners?   _____ _____

7. Are you ready to effectively utilize non-cash relationship currencies in your dealings with customers and business partners?   _____ _____

8. Are you ready to systematically value, measure, and manage currencies other than cash?   _____ _____

9. Are you ready to get the right information to the right person at the right time?   _____ _____

10. Are you ready to assess whether to iterate each relationship after every interaction?   _____ _____

It is our belief that if you answered no to *any* of our questions, you need to understand why and then identify a plan of action to answer the question with a yes. Until you can answer yes to every question, you will not realize all the benefits of collaborative business.

THE FUNDAMENTAL QUESTION

When we undertook the challenge of writing this book, we knew it would require our looking at relationships from many perspectives. We knew that to accurately describe the significance of relationships in the era of collaborative business, we had to describe the big picture. We had to describe how to value relationships on a macro level—from a company's perspective. And at the same time we knew what we were describing was such a profound change from the prevailing mindset that we also had to describe how to value relationships on a micro level—up close and personal.

We've discussed how we draw a distinction between the macro and micro views of relationships because even though people think about the relationships their company has on a company-to-company basis, relationships actually exist on a person-to-person basis. In light of this reality, we have tried to provide the understanding and the tools to answer the question, *How do you do business in the era of collaborative business?* on both levels—the micro and the macro.

Before you start the dance, let's take a few minutes to quickly review the Purposeful Collaboration Process shown in Figure 10.1. We start in the center of the figure because the technique of "Developing Understanding" underlies all nine components of Purposeful Collaboration. Assumptions are your beliefs based on your current level of understanding. As you learn from putting your assumptions into practice and then gathering, processing, and connecting new information, your level of understanding improves, and you refine your ideas and then make better assumptions. This iterative process of learning is universal and needs to become an ingrained part of how you do business.

▌ The technique of "Developing Understanding" underlies
all nine components of Purposeful Collaboration.

Now let's look at each of the nine components of the Purposeful Collaboration Process:

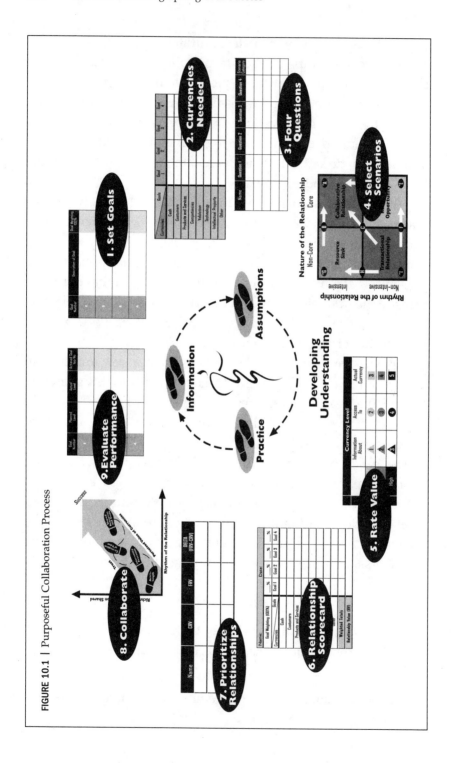

FIGURE 10.1 | Purposeful Collaboration Process

1. **Set Goals** (Figure 6.4)—Start by identifying your goals for the current period. Once you've written out your goals and identified the milestone, you'll use to assess performance, determine the relative importance of each goal and assign a weighting factor.

2. **Currencies Needed** (Figure 6.5)—Having determined your goals, identify the specific currencies you believe are necessary to help you achieve each of your goals.

3. **Four Questions** (Figure 6.6)—Now that you've identified your goals and the currencies you need, go through all of your relationships, answering the four questions about every individual.

4. **Select Scenarios** (Figure 6.2)—By answering the four questions, you can place every relationship into one of nine different relationship scenario categories. Then identify the specific Relationship Scenarios you want to dig deeper into. Remember, Scenarios A–D represent the greatest opportunity.

5. **Rate Value** (Figure 7.1)—In preparation for completing a Relationship Scorecard for each person in the identified scenarios, assess the level and utility of the currencies you believe you'll receive from each person.

6. **Relationship Scorecard** (Figure 7.2)—Using the currency value 5-point rating system, complete a current and future Relationship Scorecard for each person you evaluate.

7. **Prioritize Relationships** (Figure 7.8)—Now it's time to establish priorities. Calculating the Relationship Value Delta (Future Relationship Value – Current Relationship Value) determines the relative priority of all your relationships. The scorecard provides a wealth of information, so analyze that too.

8. **Collaborate** (Figure 8.1)—Now that you've determined with whom you want to collaborate and the specific currencies each could provide, you must build the required level of trust through the activities associated with each level of collaboration. You do this by constructing a series of value propositions that get each party successively closer to obtaining the currencies it needs to achieve its goals.

9. **Evaluate Performance** (Figure 9.5)—After every interaction, assess whether you've gained access to the desired currencies. Then, based on your analysis and your ability to see the pattern in the data, refine the value proposition, if necessary. Stand back and evaluate whether the currencies you received did, in fact, allow you to achieve your goals. During this process of evaluation, learn as much as you can about what worked and, even more important, what didn't work, so you can make better assumptions going forward. This requirement is really important because assessing the real-time progress and making changes just as soon as your intuition (fed by the data provided by the Relationship Scorecard) tells you will save you valuable resources. With this knowledge, refine your goals for the future and start the Purposeful Collaboration Process over again and again and again.

HOW YOU THINK MATTERS MOST

▐ The Relationship Matrix and the Relationship Scorecard evaluate the strategic benefit of collaborating with a specific business entity.

We've seen that the Relationship Matrix and the Relationship Scorecard are employed to evaluate the strategic benefit of collaborating with a specific business entity (individual or company) given the goals you are trying to achieve. But as we hope this book has demonstrated, the real key to collaboration is on the individual relationship (personal) level. No matter how important a collaboration may be between companies or how cleverly an agreement is structured, the collaboration will not succeed if the necessary activities on the individual level don't occur. And for activities to occur on the individual relationship level, it is important to know how you should think about relationships in the era of collaborative business.

> ▎**Collaboration will not succeed if** the necessary activities on the individual level don't occur.

Clearly, how you think matters most because it directly influences how you allocate your resources in two main ways: (1) focusing your limited resources to provide the greatest benefit and fastest return, and (2) reducing the risk of exhausting your valuable resources on wasteful resource sinks.

With the development of the Relationship Matrix and the Relationship Scorecard, we have objectified this analytical process. Indeed, we can now see the individual cells of the Relationship Scorecard as data points in the puzzle of understanding on a real-time basis whether you are making progress toward your goals and thus can take immediate action if you are not satisfied with that progress.

However, we recognize that while our challenge has been to insert systematic data collection and analysis into every facet of business relationships, it is your challenge to know when to transcend the numbers and go with your gut. After all the measurements and analyses are done, you still have to make a decision, which sometimes means going beyond the data to rely on your intuition. We don't mean we're throwing everything we've said out the window, but this book would not be completely accurate if we implied that all decisions can be turned into a purely mechanical process. They can't. But it is an old saw that the person who seems to have better intuition is usually someone who has better information. So it is vital to have access to the information that the Relationship Matrix and Relationship Scorecard provide.

❚ **The person who seems to** have better intuition usually has better information.

Thus, the implications of our new methodologies and technologies are profound. First, you can exponentially increase the level of information at your fingertips for making significant business decisions by now valuing, measuring, and managing strategic relationships at their fundamental human level. Second, you can use a broader approach that includes cash and currencies other than cash to sustain these relationships. Third, you can build collaborative business relationships that are based on trusting, purposeful, mutually beneficial value propositions.

As we've stressed throughout the book, collaborative relationships don't just happen. In addition to requiring a lot of hard work, this new repertoire of relationship skills is fundamentally different from the skill set that was required in the product-centric business environment and therefore takes time to absorb and develop. But the task must be accomplished. Why?

Because as we all know, business begins in the mind. In the age of collaborative business you must think from the perspective of everyone as a customer, that there is quantifiable and significant value in non-cash currencies, and that the intricacies of all forms of business relationships can be objectively measured and managed. By thinking about business from these new perspectives, you can understand where your business is and where it is going. This is the beginning of Purposeful Collaboration.

To be successful in the era of collaborative business
where everyone is a customer . . .
you must have the mindset of an entrepreneur and
the skillset of a choreographer.

So the time has come to put down this book, lace up your dancing shoes, and . . .

Let the dance begin!

REFERENCES

Adams, Scott. *Dilbert*. United Feature Syndicate, Inc., 12 August 2001.

Blair, Tony. Speech to Labour Party Conference, Brighton, England, 2 October 2001.

Bobby, Eric. Interview. October 2001.

Closs, David. "Collaborative Business: Competitive Advantage beyond the Enterprise." An Expert Panel Discussion hosted by J. D. Edwards, 5 October 2001.

Daly, James. "Sage Advice: An Exclusive Interview with Peter Drucker." *Business 2.0*, August 2000.

Drucker, Peter. Keynote Presentation, Delphi Group's Collaborative Commerce Summit, San Diego, CA, 4 June 2001.

———. *Innovation and Entrepreneurship*. New York: Harper and Row, 1985.

Evans, Bob. "New Century Compels Collaboration." betweenThe Lines@update.informationweek.com, 21 February 2001.

"Excerpts from President Bush's Remarks." *Boston Globe,* 12 October 2001.

Hensarling, Lenley. "Collaborative Business: Competitive Advantage beyond the Enterprise," An Expert Panel Discussion hosted by J. D. Edwards, 5 October 2001.

Kasper-Fuehrer, and Neal M. Ashkanasy. "Communicating Trustworthiness and Building Trust in Interorganizational Virtual Organizations." *Journal of Management* (May 2001).

Kawasaki, Guy. "Rules for Revolutionaries." Keynote Presentation at the Thirteenth Annual Ernst & Young Entrepreneur of the Year International Conference, Palm Desert, CA, 11 November 1999.

Kraus, Janet. Interview at Circles, Inc. October 2001 and company's Executive Summary, 14 September 2001.

McDougall, Paul. "Collaborative Business." *InformationWeek,* 7 May 2001.

Merriam-Webster's Collegiate Dictionary, 10th ed. Springfield, MA: Merriam-Webster, 2000.

Murphy, Jean V. "Forget the 'E'! C-Commerce Is the Next Big Thing." *Global Logistics & Supply Chain Strategies,* August 2001.

Pink, Daniel H. "Free Agent Nation." *Fast Company,* January 1998.

———. *Free Agent Nation.* New York: Warner Books, 2001.

———. Telephone interview, 24 October 2001.

Sawhney, Mohanbir, and Deval Parikh. "Where Value Lives in a Networked World." *Harvard Business Review* (January 2001).

Schifrin, Matthew. "Partner or Perish." *Forbes.com*, 21 May 2001.

Schrage, Michael. "Whip Your Thoroughbreds." *Fortune*, 12 November 2001 © 2001 Time Inc. All rights reserved.

Shuman, Jeffrey, with David Rottenberg. *The Rhythm of Business: The Key to Building and Running Successful Companies.* Woburn, MA: Butterworth-Heinemann, 1998.

Shuman, Jeffrey, and Janice Twombly, with David Rottenberg. *Collaborative Communities: Partnering for Profit in the Networked Economy.* Chicago: Dearborn Trade, 2001.

Varian, Hal. "Collaborative Business: Competitive Advantage beyond the Enterprise." An Expert Panel Discussion hosted by J. D. Edwards, 5 October 2001.

Watson, James K. Jr. "The Value of Collaboration." *Information-Week*, 30 July 2001.

Wilderman, Barry. "Collaborative Business: Competitive Advantage beyond the Enterprise." An Expert Panel Discussion hosted by J. D. Edwards, 5 October 2001.

White, Travis. "Collaborative Business: Competitive Advantage beyond the Enterprise." An Expert Panel Discussion hosted by J. D. Edwards, 5 October 2001.

Wong, Jason. Interview. 30 November 2001.

Zarrett, Joe. Interview at Verndale Corporation, October 2001.

<www.arthurandersen.com/webs.../MediaCenterNewsDesk DYG05092001!>

<www.britannica.com/bcom/eb/article/0/0,5716,118760+8+110116,00>

<www.dewolfe.com/CGIX/DEWWEBAS.EXE?XDWT+1AB0>

<www.hometouch.com/aboutus.cfm>

<www.wineaccess.com/bboard/q-and-a.tcl?topic=Wine>

INDEX

Jeffrey Shuman, Ph.D., and Janice Twombly are the founders of The Rhythm of Business, Inc., a Newton, Massachusetts, firm that helps businesspeople and organizations measure and manage the value in their business relationships in order to realize strategic benefit. Experts in the emerging field of collaborative business, Jeff and Jan pay particular attention to understanding the impact of advances in information and communications technologies on the relationship between a business and its customers.

Jeff is also professor and director of Bentley College's Entrepreneurial Studies Program in Waltham, Massachusetts. Bentley's award-winning program is based on the iterative and intuitive business-building process first described in Jeff's book *The Rhythm of Business: The Key to Building and Running Successful Companies* (Butterworth-Heinemann, 1998). Bentley's program is among the top 25 entrepreneurship programs, according to the 2002 *U.S. News & World Report* rankings. Jeff has been part of the founding team of six companies in diverse industries, ranging from manufacturing and distribution to software development. He has served as advisor, consultant, and educator to thousands of businesspeople throughout his career.

Jan has worked with entrepreneurs and free agents in the earliest stages of their businesses, consulted with established companies, and served as president of a company that produced and marketed educational business conferences and publications for manufacturers adopting collaborative product development practices. She is a Certified Public Accountant and was formerly a partner and human resources director with a regional CPA firm. She serves on the boards of directors of RelationsWeb and Responsible World, Inc. Jan has also served on the boards of not-for-profit organizations that promote entrepreneurship as a means out of poverty for women, and she was a delegate to the 1997 Microcredit Summit.

David Rottenberg is the editor for The Rhythm of Business, Inc. He has also worked as a freelance author and has written business profiles for *Boston Magazine* as well as articles for several national computer publications.

The Rhythm of Business, Inc., provides education and training offerings, publications, consulting, and software products that offer the understanding and tools required for the development and implementation of collaborative business models, processes, and relationships that can iterate as customers and the business environment change. For more information, visit us at <www.rhythmofbusiness.com>.

EVERYONE IS A CUSTOMER

Now your entire organization can learn
how to grow "customer" relationships!
For quantities of *Everyone Is a Customer,*
please contact Mindi Rowland in
Special Sales, 800-621-9621, ext. 4410,
rowland@dearborn.com.

Your company also can order
this book with a
customized cover featuring
your name, logo, and message.

Dearborn™
Trade Publishing
A **Kaplan Professional** Company